Your Special Education Rights

Your Special Education Rights

What Your School District Isn't Telling You

JENNIFER LAVIANO AND JULIE SWANSON

Skyhorse Publishing

Skyhorse Publishing books may be purchased in bulk at special discounts for sales promotion, corporate gifts, fund-raising, or educational purposes. Special editions can also be created to specifications. For details, contact the Special Sales Department, Skyhorse Publishing, 307 West 36th Street, 11th Floor, New York, NY 10018 or info@skyhorsepublishing.com.

Skyhorse® and Skyhorse Publishing® are registered trademarks of Skyhorse Publishing, Inc.®, a Delaware corporation.

Visit our website at www.skyhorsepublishing.com.

10 9 8 7 6 5 4 3

Library of Congress Cataloging-in-Publication Data is available on file.

Cover design by Rain Saukas
Front cover illustration: iStockphoto

Print ISBN: 978-1-5107-1939-2
Ebook ISBN: 978-1-5107-1940-8

Printed in the United States of America

Most people see what is, and never see what can be.
—Albert Einstein

This book is dedicated to those who see what their child can be.

Contents

A Note from the Authors

We've written this book primarily for parents. However, one of the things we always say when we present to parent groups is this: "We know we're jaded." Parents often hire us when their child is in a crisis, or when their relationship with their child's school has reached a point where they no longer feel able to communicate without a professional advocate or attorney. That is *not* the norm! Given that, we would like to say a word to educators and administrators who are reading this book. We came close to naming this book *Your Special Education Rights: What You Don't Know Can Hurt You.* However, we felt that title placed the blame for not understanding their rights on parents, which we did not think was entirely fair. After all, Congress requires school districts to inform parents of their rights. We, therefore, then came awfully close to the title: *Your Special Education Rights: What Your School District Won't Tell You.* But that seemed too harsh as well. We ultimately decided to emphasize that schools *may not* tell parents certain things, rather than assuming that they won't.

We realize that highlighting what school districts might not tell parents may have the unintended consequence of leaving educators and administrators with the impression that we have written this book to "bash" school districts. We did not. In fact, we are both products of public education, and we believe in it, strongly! We recognize that the vast majority of people who choose to become teachers do so because they love children and care about education. We believe that most administrators are trying their best under enormous financial, political, and legal pressure. Our sincere hope is that our candid account does not alienate educators and administrators, but rather raises awareness of how difficult it can be to navigate the special education system. Our goal is empowerment of parents so that they can work shoulder to shoulder with their school districts on behalf of their child, rather than against them.

In addition to wanting you to consider that our perspective is one that is very much colored by the unfortunate nature of the cases in which we are involved, it is imperative that you read this book knowing that, in the law, and in the world in which we live, things are *constantly* changing. As this book was heading to print, a number of events happened on the national scene that made us realize we would be remiss to allow the book to be published without addressing them. The 2016 election represents a major "shift" in the philosophy of the role that the federal government should play in education at both the executive and legislative branches. The Individuals with Disabilities Education Act (IDEA) and Section 504 of the Rehabilitation Act of 1973, the key federal protections for students with disabilities, are enforced through federal agencies and private actions by parents. How a dramatic change in these agencies will impact special education advocacy remains unknown. A renewed focus on states' rights versus federal oversight, and an emphasis on vouchers in education, will change the landscape of special education in ways that are worrisome to many.

Further, on March 22, 2017, the United States Supreme Court issued its ruling in the *Endrew F. v. Douglas County*

School District case. Endrew F. is a student identified for special education services as a result of an autism spectrum disorder, whose parents removed him from a public school program they believed was inappropriate and placed him in a private special education school for which they sought reimbursement. This was the first time in thirty-five years that the High Court had considered the question of what an "appropriate" program is under the IDEA, the federal law that requires that children who are identified as eligible to receive special education services as a result of their disabilities receive a "free appropriate public education" (FAPE) from their school districts annually. In striking down a Tenth Circuit decision holding that the IDEA requires that students receive "educational benefit [that is] merely . . . more than *de minimis,*" the court found that the IDEA requires far more. In invoking the history of what led Congress to enact the IDEA to begin with in 1975, the *Endrew F.* court noted that a proper analysis of whether a child's Individualized Education Program (IEP) is "appropriate" under the law *must* consider the individual and unique needs of the child, and further must be focused on that student's progress: "A substantive standard not focused on student progress would do little to remedy the pervasive and tragic academic stagnation that prompted Congress to act." Citing the need for "ambitious" goals, and focusing on the need for individualization in the special education programming, the court held: "When all is said and done, a student offered an educational program providing 'merely more than *de minimis*' progress from year to year can hardly be said to have been offered an education at all. For children with disabilities, receiving instruction that aims so low would be tantamount to 'sitting idly . . . awaiting the time when they were old enough to 'drop out.' *Rowley*, 458 US, at 179. The IDEA demands more. It requires an educational program reasonably calculated to enable a child to make progress appropriate in light of the child's circumstances."

How this landmark decision will be interpreted by hearing officers and courts remains to be seen. There does appear to be a consensus in the legal community that the decision marks a higher standard than the court had previously articulated, and that substandard education for children with disabilities does not pass legal muster. As importantly, the court continually brings the analysis back to focusing on the unique needs of the child in question.

Finally, we also think it's worth saying a few words about the chapter we have included on Sandy Hook. We debated it between ourselves and with colleagues, friends, and our publisher. At no point did we want to be exploitative of the horror experienced by the families; in no way did we want to feed into a false perception that individuals with disabilities are inherently violent, dangerous, or unstable; and candidly, we didn't want to invite a controversial subject into a book that already reveals difficult truths about the inner workings of school systems.

And yet, we could not help but conclude that we must address Sandy Hook, as difficult and sensitive as the topic is. You will learn from that chapter that Connecticut's Office of the Child Advocate found that there was a failure on the part of the Newtown Public Schools to follow the IDEA with regard to Adam Lanza, though of course neither the OCA, nor we, are claiming that this, or any one factor, was the "single causation" for the tragedy. The lessons from Sandy Hook were especially compelling to us since, all of these years later, while Newtown itself has made significant, positive changes in its special education administration and the professional advice it obtains in numerous domains, we continue to see schools that do not take the precautions we would hope they would.

Our public school educators are on the "front line" of identifying students whose behaviors may be troubling, and yet so many of them fail to refer students to special education because they continue to operate under the misguided and legally untenable belief that if a kid is "smart," they aren't entitled to special education services, or because they underestimate the special education services that a child may require beyond academics. Having said that, we have seen many schools that do their best to identify and service students with complex profiles. We hope our decision to incorporate a chapter on this incredibly difficult topic is instructive and preventive.[1]

We have written this book for parents as our primary intended audience. Yet, parents, educators, and administrators are all in this together. We don't know what *your* child needs or how *your* school district operates. Our goals are for parents to have the information they need and to be aware that there is important information that their school district may not be telling them that can make a difference in their advocacy, and ultimately, in their child's life.

---

1   Many thanks go to our colleague and friend, Attorney Andrew Feinstein. The chapter on Sandy Hook grew from a presentation Andy and Jen prepared for the national conference of COPAA, the Council of Parent Attorneys and Advocates, in 2014.

Introduction: The One/Two Punch

It was the mid-1990s. Jen was a brand-new, fresh out of the box attorney, working in her father's civil rights law office. Bill Laviano was a force to be reckoned with: a four-hundred-pound Italian-American litigator with a graying beard and a brain too big for most people to manage and an ego to match. Julie's son had just been diagnosed with autism (at a time when few people knew what it was or talked about it). She and her husband were looking for an applied behavioral analysis (ABA) program for their son, a particular methodology that back then was virtually unheard of in public schools. Only one case had been litigated in Connecticut for such a program. They hired Bill and began a hard, acrimonious legal battle with their town.

Several days into the due process hearing, a scheduling conflict arose. Everyone was available for a hearing date except Bill. "No problem," he said. "I can send my daughter Jenny." Julie and her husband exchanged worried looks. They asked to speak with Bill outside the hearing room, where they expressed their concerns about having their son's case handed over to someone they'd never met, who they'd never heard of, in the middle of the case.

Bill didn't take it well. He was a man who would take on city hall, state and federal governments, the Catholic church, the state police, and virtually any company or institution without flinching, but an attack on any of his four daughters could level him in an instant. How dare Julie and her husband question the capability of his daughter? He took their check for several thousand dollars and ripped it up in front of their faces. Julie and her husband were speechless, but knew they had to accept this unknown young lawyer for a day of the hearing or try to find another law firm mid-trial.

Jen was less than thrilled to hear her father's solution. He'd thrown her into more than a few of these difficult situations in the few months since she'd been sworn into the bar, and despite his efforts to convince her that Julie and her husband were in the wrong, Jen knew better. They had every reason to be furious, she told her father, and by the way, thanks so much!

This is how Jen and Julie met. They hit it off immediately.

Fast-forward more than a decade. Bill has passed away, and Jen has continued working as a civil rights lawyer, focusing her practice entirely on special education cases. Julie has become a successful professional advocate, working with families to secure appropriate special education services. She also tries to bring disabilities to the media's attention, but has faced an uphill battle, becoming outraged when one of the producers on a local news station told her that "our audience just isn't interested in disabilities."

Julie is not a woman who takes "no" for an answer.

That's when it dawned on her: she needed someone to pair up with in her advocacy work who could provide legal expertise to fight the bias she continued to encounter. She needed a lawyer. And she just happened to know one.

Julie pursued Jen for two years, trying to convince her to join forces with her. Jen was reluctant—too busy and sure that if people wanted to hear from a lawyer they'd hire one—but Julie was persistent. She finally convinced Jen by saying, "I'm the parent, you're the lawyer, together we're the one/two punch!"

With Jen on board, they worked together, doing everything from radio interviews to blogging, and ultimately created an award-winning video-based website called YourSpecialEducationRights.com. Their mission is to make sure that parents of children with disabilities know their rights, and can apply them, so that the outcomes for those kids dramatically improve.

And what happened with Julie's case? She ultimately prevailed, her son received an excellent program for his educational years, and he is now thriving in the adult world.

Part 1: What Your School District Isn't Telling You

It all seems very simple. A special education law, the Individuals with Disabilities Education Act (IDEA), was enacted by Congress in 1975 (originally called the Education for All Handicapped Children Act) to ensure that children with disabilities have the opportunity to receive a free appropriate public education, just like other children.

But nothing is ever simple.

At least once a day, a parent we represent asks us, "Why would they do that? It doesn't make any sense." Sometimes, the decisions that school districts make *don't* make sense. In those cases, we remind our clients that you can't use logic to talk someone out of a position they didn't use logic to get into.

However, more often than not, there are reasons for what may seem like totally arbitrary decision making. It's just that those reasons are unknown to most parents, who don't have the benefit of dealing with numerous school districts every single day. When you have that perspective, as we do, you start to realize that there are multiple agendas and competing interests operating within a school district that motivate the decisions made at Individualized Education Program (IEP) meetings. (IEPs are legally required documents, generated by a team of educators and the parents of the child, which serve almost like a contract between the school and the parents. They outline what the school intends to provide the child.) This perspective includes understanding that each of the educators has her own perspective, job, role, and sometimes, fears. As a parent, you would understand why someone responded a certain way at your child's meeting if you knew that one of the people there is another person's direct supervisor. Or that regular education teachers often don't feel the same pressure to follow the orders of the special education administrator as someone who reports directly to that administrator. Or that the behind-the-scenes politics of the building are influencing how the educators around that table are interacting with one another. Or that the way your state sets up certain funding mechanisms is, in fact, a huge barrier to getting what you want at the meeting. But nobody around the table is likely to tell you all of this.

Let's use an example from our state to illustrate what we mean. In Connecticut, as in most states, our Department of Education has a process of approving private special education schools, which thereby authorizes it to provide special education services to students who have IEPs. The state maintains a list of approved programs, and school districts can place students at these programs through their IEPs. Connecticut also has a funding structure for school districts whereby the state will contribute significant monies to a child's program if the district goes over their "excess cost threshold" for that student. Basically, the state will defray costs for a student whose program becomes extremely expensive. But here's the kicker: the state will *only* defray those costs if the program the child is attending is on the state approved list. It will not contribute to a private special education program that is not approved by the state. Connecticut, like many states, has a number of private special education schools that elect to remain independent. Those schools aren't on the approved list. Therefore, the districts can't get the excess costs for them covered.

This funding structure can have really strange results. We've seen cases where a child is placed at a non-approved, private special education school, and is thriving. The district team members observe the child and agree the program is the perfect fit for him. The parents agree that program is the appropriate program for him. Everyone on the IEP team says, "Yes, this is the right school for him." But because the school is not on the approved list, the district denies the request for the placement (and subsequent funding), instead offering an approved program that is even more expensive than the non-approved program! Rightly so, the parents say, "Everyone agrees this is the right school and that he's doing beautifully there, but the answer is no?" The IEP team in this case is making a decision that defies logic—until you understand that the state is pulling the strings here just like Oz behind the curtain.

Once you understand the hidden motivators and obstacles to special education decision making in public schools, the seemingly mysterious answers you have been getting will start to make sense.

1

Your Special Education Director May Not Know Who You Are

Many parents assume that, simply because their child has a disability, the Director of Special Education in their district is aware of the case. That is just not so, especially in a larger district. It would be impossible for one administrator to be aware of every child with a disability in, say, Los Angeles or Chicago. Even in much smaller cities than that, usually there is a structure of administration, and the Special Education Director entrusts her team to handle the day-to-day obligations of the district to the children in each building. In many cases, there are building-level administrators who are responsible for convening special education meetings; sometimes they aren't even special educators! For this reason, we strongly advocate that parents find out who the Director of Special Education is in their district, and work toward meeting and ultimately building a relationship with her.

Directors manage a very large budget. In many school systems, the director reports directly to the superintendent, and in most systems, the Director of Special Education is a district-wide administrator. This means that your child's building principal is *under* the Director of Special Education, not the other way around. According to SalaryExpert.com, the average special education director in the United States makes $94,184.00 per year. That's an *average*. In many states, directors of special education make well over six figures a year. It's an important job, and it should be.

And yet, we have found that some special education administrators do not have even a basic understanding of their legal obligations. In some situations, this means that they are failing to follow the procedures outlined by federally mandated regulations. In others, it means that if a parent brings in a non-attorney advocate to an IEP meeting, the district brings in its lawyer because the director doesn't know how to navigate the complex laws involving special education.

Think about that: in these cases, parents are expected to go up against an administrator who has at her disposal an attorney to bring in when things get even a little bit complex. That should tell you something about how imbalanced the power between parents and their school districts can be and often is. Unless a parent has the means and ability to hire a lawyer or good non-attorney advocate, he will be facing a Herculean task in the event of a legal dispute.

Let us give you just one example of where we see administrators making a basic legal error that will ultimately cost their district far more than if they understood the law. The IDEA states that a parent has the right to ask for an Independent Educational Evaluation (IEE) if they disagree with their school district's testing. If the parent asks for the IEE, the district has the right to say no, and refuse the evaluation at public expense. However, if it does that, it must, without delay, file for a due process hearing defending its own testing before a hearing officer. (Read more about IEEs in chapter 14.) This is a requirement under federal law. Yet many directors have no idea that they are required to file for a hearing, even when we tell them so. They simply say no to the IEE and then do nothing. Eventually, many of these parents figure out that the district was required to act when it denied the request, and at that point, if the director is getting even decent legal advice, the school district will just go ahead and pay for the outside evaluation. But by then, the district is incurring legal fees on top of the IEE, as well as eroding the faith and trust of the parents in the competence of the district.

Wouldn't it be better if the director knew what she should have done the first time around?

As we have acknowledged, we have a very cynical view of many issues because of the nature of the cases we see. However, we do know that the Director of Special Education is typically the person with the most authority in your district to make decisions about your child's special education program. Unless you plan on moving out of your school system, you may be working with this person for many, many years. Building a good, respectful, cooperative relationship with him early on in your child's education may make an enormous difference in the outcomes for your child.

If you are in the unfortunate position of residing in a district where your Director of Special Education is not discharging her obligations in accordance with the law, speak up! Make your district hold your director accountable for its obligations to students with disabilities. Go to your school board meetings, point out the problems, and ask administrators to fix them. Ask for regularly scheduled annual training on the IDEA, Section 504, and other legal obligations of school districts, and continuing education for the director and all educators, staff, and administration.

2

Who's Chairing the Meeting, Anyway?

We often receive phone calls from parents right after the wrong decision has been made for their child at an IEP team meeting.

Among the first questions we ask parents is, "Who was chairing the IEP meeting?" All too often parents don't know the answer to this simple question. It's important to know the answer and here's why. The IDEA is clear about the specific roles that must be filled at an IEP team meeting for your child. In fact, on the list of required members of the IEP team is "a representative of the public agency [usually the school district] who is qualified to provide, or supervise the provision of, specially designed instruction to meet the unique needs of children with disabilities; is knowledgeable about the general education curriculum; and is knowledgeable about the availability of resources of the public agency."

This should be the person who is chairing the meeting because he is knowledgeable about the availability of resources of the public agency. Should available resources drive all decisions? Of course not. But it's critical to know that money factors into the decision making process (so much so that we devoted chapter 3 to it). Key decisions live and die over the resources available to the school district. Your school district carefully protects its resources and knows exactly just how far they can be stretched before they impact the special education budget.

Back to the point about who's chairing the meeting. This is one of those requirements of the IDEA that is often not followed and, unfortunately, can impact the outcome of a meeting and services for a student.

So here's the bottom line. Pay attention to who is chairing the meeting on the invitation you receive. Every school district is different, so this person may be referred to as the administrator, supervisor, chair, or coordinator. Confirm that this person—regardless of title—is knowledgeable about the district's resources.

There are other required members of the IEP team meeting as well:

a. *General.* The public agency [usually your school district] must ensure that the IEP team for each child with a disability includes:

1. The parents of the child
2. Not less than one regular education teacher of the child (if the child is, or may be, participating in the regular education environment)
3. Not less than one special education teacher of the child, or where appropriate, not less than one special education provider of the child
4. A representative of the public agency who:

      i. Is qualified to provide, or supervise the provision of, specially designed instruction to meet the unique needs of children with disabilities

      ii. Is knowledgeable about the general education curriculum

      iii. Is knowledgeable about the availability of resources of the public agency

5. An individual who can interpret the instructional implications of evaluation results, who may be a member of the team described in paragraphs (a)(2) through (a)(6) of this section

6. At the discretion of the parent or the agency, other individuals who have knowledge or special expertise regarding the child, including related services personnel as appropriate

7. Whenever appropriate, the child with a disability

What Your School District Isn't Telling You

Chances are that the school team is not going to tell you who is authorized in your district to allocate funds and other resources. Why not? Money; the staff may change; or they may not realize that parents are unaware of who makes these decisions in their district. So how do you figure it out? A good place to start is with the notice of the meeting, which is typically the written invitation you get to the IEP meeting. If you're reading this and asking yourself, "What invitation?", you've got bigger problems, because the IDEA requires that school districts inform you of the IEP meeting in writing, including who is invited to attend, what their roles are, and what the purpose of the meeting is. You must receive a written notice in advance of the IEP team meeting. Check the number of days of advance notice the state requires that you must be given to receive it prior to the meeting; your school district isn't legally permitted to just spring an IEP meeting on you without giving you advance notice, and usually enough time to prepare. Pay attention to the invitation. You may be expecting someone to attend who is not on the invitation, or someone is on the invitation you don't know. Reviewing the invitation attendees prior to the meeting allows you to ask questions if something seems off to you, or to ask your school to invite someone they have left out.

The purpose of the meeting is another very important section of the invitation to review. We've often seen parents request the IEP meeting due to their concerns, and the invitation purpose does not reflect that. Checking the stated purpose of the IEP meeting *before* attending gives you the opportunity to set the record straight, or alerts you if the team is calling the meeting for a reason you don't understand or are worried about, such as to plan an evaluation. If the invitation is not accurate, request a corrected notice in writing. Make sure you let the school know that the corrected invitation does not have to reset the date of the meeting. If you were not able to correct the notice, or didn't realize it was in error prior to the meeting, put it at the top of the agenda at the meeting, simply by stating, "I want to correct the IEP meeting notice (or invitation)," and then indicating what is in error. If the only chance you get to correct the notice or invitation is in the meeting itself, ask that a corrected notice or invitation be sent to you after the meeting.

Again, who's chairing the meeting? We've seen thousands of IEP meeting notices, and it's not always clear. It may list a "chair," but it often includes a spot for "administrative designee" or similar category. This does not mean, however, that this person is officially blessed by the district to make all financial and resource allocation decisions. As a legal matter, the IEP team is supposed to be fully authorized to commit resources to the child, but this is not always the way it works, especially in larger districts. Educators who don't believe they are permitted by their bosses to commit district funds often won't. If you suspect, based on the IEP meeting notice/invitation, that no one who has been invited to the meeting has the ability to commit the resources of the district, ask before the meeting, in writing, to have the appropriate person invited.

What You Can Do about It

Pen a polite email that goes something like this:

> Dear (insert chairperson),
>
> I am in receipt of the invitation to the IEP team meeting for my son/daughter, (insert name), on (insert date). It is my understanding that in your role as the chairperson of the IEP team meeting, you are knowledgeable about the availability of resources of the district. I wanted to confirm that, with you as chair, the IEP team will be authorized to commit district resources. Is this accurate? If not, will a person who is in that role be able to attend the

13

IEP team meeting in addition to yourself? If not, could that person be available during the meeting by phone?

Include this part if it has actually happened to you in the past:

I have attended previous IEP meeting(s) where the chair has informed me that he/she was not authorized to commit district resources without permission of another administrator who wasn't at the meeting. I hope you can appreciate that I am trying to avoid this situation from happening again.

Thank you so much for letting me know in writing prior to the IEP team meeting that all necessary members will be present.

Many thanks,

(insert your name)
cc: Director of Special Education

3

They Care about Money. A Lot.

There are so many quotes about how important money is that it's almost impossible to list them: "Money makes the world go 'round." "Follow the money." "Show me the money!" Yes, money matters.

We all like to think of our children's schools as kind places where you bring the teachers apples. And many of them are. But they are also governmental agencies. They are also entities that have budgets. If you think that money is not influencing the decisions made around the table, you are being incredibly naive. Does this mean that money is the sole motivating factor? Of course not. But the cold hard facts are these: children with disabilities require services. Services cost money. The more complex the child, the costlier the program. Period.

You may already know this if you pay any attention to your board of education's budget discussions, wherein special education is almost always cited as a scapegoat. But you still may not understand *how* budgetary considerations are influencing the IEP team's decisions. It's not always as obvious as you might think. Here are some ways in which money is factoring into the decisions your school district is making about your child:

1. Evaluations

Federal law requires that students who are suspected of having a disability be evaluated, and if found eligible for special education services, reevaluated at least every three years. These evaluations are typically performed by the school district staff: school psychologists, special education teachers, speech pathologists, occupational therapists, and so on. The evaluation is required to assess the student in "all suspected areas of disability," and further, the testing is supposed to take into consideration numerous factors. So how can something as simple as having your child tested by his own school team be subject to the influences of money? Well, let's start with the tests themselves. Standardized tests are published and copyrighted, and require training. In order to administer them, the district has to buy them. Do you think most school districts buy every single instrument that is out there to test, let's say, IQ? Of course not! They buy one, maybe two protocols, and whoever is testing the child's cognitive ability in the school is likely going to use one of those two. So right out of the gate of the testing of this child, the district is almost always going to be using the tests it has, rather than really sitting down and considering whether there are other instruments available to purchase that might be more appropriate to use to assess this particular child. If your child is more complex than the average child with a disability, this can have a huge impact on the test results.

In addition to just which tests are used, evaluation results are often tainted by money in the following way: the recommendations for services, hours of instruction,

16

type of programming, and placement are being made by employees of the school district. Let that sink in. This means that the results of the testing, and the recommendations that flow from the data gleaned, are going to be made by a person who has to decide whether to put in writing that this child requires a service that is going to cost the school district money. It's as simple as that. Do we believe that the evaluators who are testing our public school kids every day are cold-hearted, calculating individuals who are intentionally skewing their recommendations in order to save their school district money? No, we don't. We do know, however, that educators are under enormous pressure in some subtle and not so subtle ways to keep the resources of the district in mind when they make their recommendations. (See chapter 4 for more information.) This is a sad reality that you need to understand.

2. Staffing

For each school, there is a staff. Each of those staff members comes at a cost to the district. We all understand this. But staffing impacts special education decisions in ways you might not think.

Parents often ask why a district will deny additional service hours for speech therapy, for example. Presumably that denial is simply because the team doesn't believe the child needs it. We can grant that. However, you might want to know the answer to the following question: Is the speech pathologist on contract or a salaried employee? If she is a salaried employee, whether she has a case load of ten students or twenty may be totally irrelevant to the district from a purely financial perspective. However, if the district contracts out with their speech pathologist, and by that contract, every hour of service is an additional cost, you want to know that when asking for the additional time. Same goes for outside consultants. Most have detailed contracts with the school systems they serve that cap the students or services at a certain amount, after which the district will be charged.

Let's take paraprofessionals. Many parents believe that their child requires a full-time, 1:1 aide with them throughout the day, and are perplexed as to why the district will instead offer a part-time para. It could be that this is all the child needs. However, it also may be strongly budget related. The district may only have a certain number of full-time professionals that they are approved to hire per the budget; therefore, they might assign two part-time paraprofessionals to the child throughout the day, rather than hiring a full-time person who will perform essentially the same function. While there are some good, pedagogical reasons to assign more than one paraprofessional to a student, wouldn't you want to be aware of whether or not cost was a factor when you were discussing it with your team?

3. Placement decisions

One of the most important decisions an IEP team must make is "placement." This is easily understood as "where is the child going to go to school?" In which school and/ or program will the student be placed? Just as with evaluations, this decision can be heavily connected to funding.

18

Most students with disabilities can and should be educated in the public school they would attend if they did not have a disability. However, the IDEA requires that a continuum of appropriate alternative placements be available to students. In essence, a child is supposed to be placed in the program that meets her unique needs. Here is the reality, though. Districts create programs. They create classrooms. They do so based on numbers. If a district has expended significant resources to develop a program for students who require a smaller environment to address behavior and a student comes along who requires a smaller environment for reasons other than behavior, which is more likely? That the district will create and fund an entirely new program for that one student, or that they will recommend placement for that one student in the program they already have? Again, money can be a huge consideration here.

Money particularly becomes a barrier if a parent is requesting an out-of-district, private special education placement. These programs tend to be very costly because they are usually smaller, have a better student-to-teacher ratio, and are (hopefully) taught by professionals who are highly trained in complex disabilities. Facilities and equipment in some of these programs can be very costly. For many school districts, funding a private, out-of-district placement is not something they will easily consider. Indeed, we have been told by several educators that they have been given explicit instructions by the administration to *never* approve an out-of-district placement at an IEP team meeting. Placing a child with disabilities in a school other than the one they would typically attend if they did not have a disability *should* be a decision only reached after enormous consideration, but we want you to be aware that cost is often a large factor.

Again, this is where understanding what is motivating your team matters. Another example illustrates the point: a student's medical needs are so great that the IEP team determines her needs cannot be met in the public school. The parents have looked at the programs available for such students, as has the district. The parents request School A. The district proposes School B. They cost the same. They are the same distance away. The programs are very similar. But the district is adamant that they will only agree to School B, not the parents' preference of School A. Why?

This may explain the decision: the district already has a bus going to School B. They do not have a bus going to School A. Putting together the transportation for one student to go to such a school can cost a district tens of thousands of dollars. This placement decision was clearly impacted by budget, and yet the parent would usually leave the IEP table frustrated, perplexed, and angry, without understanding the reason why.

Congress requires that students receive special education programs that are *free* and appropriate. This means "at no cost" to the parents. If a student requires a service in order to receive the appropriate special education program to which they are entitled, cost is not supposed to be a factor. However, as you can plainly see, money is often on the mind of at least the administrator in the meeting, and you would be well served to think how money might impact your requests so you are prepared to address any resistance.

What Your School District Isn't Telling You

Your school district will not necessarily tell you how much money or how many resources they have to allocate to your child's program. However, you have a right to ask how much is being spent on your individual child, and can make that request in writing. Almost every state has a procedure whereby school districts annually outline the costs for each child with an IEP, and if your school district submits this information to the state about your child, you have a right to know what it says.

In addition to information about your individual child, though, you have a right to information about the costs of special education in general in your district. The school district is accountable to the public, and must report on the state of the district's business through their annual reporting mechanism (for example, the written annual report and the budget process). Federal and state laws require public entities to be transparent to the public through "sunshine laws," and this is why you can find details about your school district's financial decisions.

You would be surprised what you can learn by going to the board meetings, watching them online or on cable television, or reading the summary of the meetings in your local newspaper. School districts are required to maintain minutes of their board meetings; those are often easy to find on your school district's website, and you should get in the habit of

21

reading them. Many board of education members are well aware of the district's legal obligations under the IDEA, and support special education earnestly. Some of these members are parents of children with disabilities who decided to create change by running for this office. Unfortunately, this is not a universal experience. Some individuals on school boards, you may find, are anti–special education and view the costs of special education as a drain or a necessary evil. These individuals are often very public about their views in this regard. We have had many cases where parents were able to prove that the motivation behind an IEP team's decision was financial, simply because a rogue board member publicly stated this in a meeting! We have also seen numerous offensive, or at best insensitive, comments made publicly by board of education members about children with disabilities. While we cringe each time it happens, we are also aware that cases are sometimes resolved because the administration realizes that such attitudes are unacceptable and would be frowned upon by a hearing officer or court. But you won't know about these attitudes unless you're paying attention.

What You Can Do about It

If the IEP team members discuss money or the cost of a service at the IEP team meeting, especially if the expenditure has been denied, it's important for you to politely call them out on it. You can say something like, "I can see that you've decided to discuss the cost of the service I've requested. It is my understanding that we are supposed to be deciding what my child requires regardless of cost. I would like to give you the opportunity to stop considering the cost of the services that might be necessary for my child to receive an appropriate program. If not, I am going to request that the record reflect my concern that the team has considered the cost of this service as a determining factor in the denial of our request for it. We are quite concerned that cost has been a determining factor in your decision."

Knowing that a decision was made based on cost may compel you to file a complaint with your state. Your state should have a complaint form or process available on their website. If you have documented that your child's IEP team denied a service because of the cost, you might want to write a complaint that details how cost was the determining factor in denying a requested program, service(s), evaluation, or placement decision at your child's IEP team meeting. It may be a good idea to call your state's Department of Education first to chat with a person in the complaint unit to see if they think your complaint has merit. We suggest this for two reasons. First, many of the people who work in the complaint units at state Departments of Education will try to rectify a situation informally if it's clear that the district has violated the IDEA, and will call the special education administration in your district and urge them to fix the problem before formal action is taken (saving you time and stress); and second, if the state representatives sound like they're not taking your concern seriously, this could foreshadow how your complaint will be decided. We are *not* saying you should withhold the filing of a complaint just because the person you spoke to doesn't sound like they are giving your concerns merit. You still have rights, and we want you to exercise them. But a bad vibe after a call to the state may inform you on how to proceed; at minimum, it justifies picking up the phone and calling a parent-side special education lawyer (someone who represents parents, generally speaking, not school districts) in your state for her advice. If you submit a complaint and your state deems it unfounded, you will have made a bad situation worse, which we don't want you to do. So proceed with extreme caution.

What can you do? Educate yourself about what goes on in your district as it specifically relates to special education funding and spending. Do what we suggested before: attend board meetings if you can or watch them on TV or online. You might be surprised what you learn about your district and how it ticks. Get to know the reporter for your local paper who covers school board meetings; he is often a font of information.

If you have discovered, or discover in the future, that your board of education misunderstands its legal obligations under the IDEA and seems to think that funding special education is optional, you have the perfect opportunity to gather a group of parents and insist that the school board receive yearly training on understanding their legal obligations under the IDEA. Or, better yet, run for the board of education yourself! We need more parents of children who receive special education on the boards making decisions about it.

4

Teachers Need to Eat, Too

We have friends who are regular education teachers, special education teachers, speech and language pathologists, board certified behavior analysts, psychologists, occupational therapists, and more. They tell us stuff. But we get most of our insight through our forty years of combined experience around the IEP table and through parents. Occasionally school staff will speak to us.

How many times have we walked out of a school after a meeting and a staff member discretely approached us and whispered, "Thank you" or "I'm sorry" or rolled their eyes as if to say, "Yeah, that was a train wreck"? Parents also tell us when they retain us that a teacher or other staff member revealed a damaging truth to them. Parents tell us they can't throw the teacher under the bus because they could lose their job. Yes, it's the whistle blower syndrome.

We've learned how things can go down in irresponsible districts. Again, we know we are cynical, and that we are involved in the cases that represent the situations in which the system is not working; but in some schools, the pressure on teachers by administration is enormous. We firmly believe that most educators, including administrators, entered the field of education because they want to help children. But there are "bad apples" in every field, including this one. The following are examples of situations that occur if you happen to have an administration focused on money, rather than children.

A speech and language pathologist may know that a student requires daily, half-hour speech sessions but can only recommend two per week because his Director of Special Education has told him not to overburden the speech and language resources of the district.

A second grade student is struggling to make reading progress. The regular education teacher desperately wants to refer the student to special education because he suspects an underlying learning disability. The district has instructed all teachers to try a Scientific Research-Based Intervention (SRBI)—a regular education initiative designed to help students who are struggling—before referring a student to special education. SRBI may be appropriate for many students, but for others it is not. Unfortunately, SRBI is often misused and/or students can be lost in this model for years without ever being referred to special education. For example, some teachers are directed to have the student go through all three tiers of SRBI before referring her to special education, as if it were a rule. There is no such rule. This type of urban legend (see chapter 21) can educationally harm a child and dramatically change the outcome of her education.

Another struggling reader in special education has a special education teacher who believes with her heart and soul that her student requires a reading program called Orton-Gillingham because the approach she is using with him is not working. The teacher calls the Director of Special Education and lets her know she would like to recommend it at the upcoming

IEP team meeting. She is swiftly told no. Meanwhile, the parent has learned about Orton-Gillingham and discussed it with the teacher. The parent requests Orton-Gillingham at the IEP team meeting. The request is denied. When the parent asks the teacher about her opinion about Orton-Gillingham, she is forced to support the current program.

We could give you lots of other examples, but we think you get the point. The fact is that there are some administrators who have adopted a culture of denying services to children with disabilities. In such situations, if teachers and other school staff want to keep their jobs, and let's face it, most of them do, they need to fall in line with what they are directed to do. No one wants to lose their job and jeopardize putting food on the table. We all have to do what our bosses tell us to do if we want to keep our jobs. But children's educations are not widgets. The right or wrong decision can change the direction of a student's life and determine the outcome for adulthood. Decisions impact whether a student goes to college or not. Decisions determine whether a child will be nonverbal or verbal. Decisions impact whether behaviors will forever become a barrier for employment. We're in the business of changing the shape of lives. Toeing the company line can be costly to students.

So what are teachers and other school staff to do? Well, that's up to them. We are fairly certain that if either of us worked for a school district that has a culture like the one we have described above, we would have been fired because we're not exactly toe-the-company-line types.

Remember that teachers have rights under Section 504 and other state-specific laws that protect them from retaliation, and we encourage the public policy consideration of advocating for children with disabilities. And don't forget that little thing called tenure.

If you are an educator, we want you to know that you have allies in us. And not just us individually. The community of parent attorneys and advocates stands shoulder-to-shoulder with those brave teachers who speak up at IEP team meetings in a school where they've been pressured not to. We remember you and wish there were more like you.

What Your School District Isn't Telling You

Your school district won't tell you that teachers and other school staff members have rights. Among those rights is the right to be free from retaliation by their employer if they are honest about what children with disabilities require. If they knew their rights, they might be more inclined to advocate for your child. School staff should know this:

Retaliation or coercion:

a. No private or public entity shall discriminate against any individual because that individual has opposed any act or practice made unlawful by this part, or because that individual made a charge, testified, assisted, or participated in any manner in an investigation, proceeding, or hearing under the Act or this part.

b. No private or public entity shall coerce, intimidate, threaten, or interfere with any individual in the exercise or enjoyment of, or on account of his or her having exercised or enjoyed, or on account of his or her having

28

aided or encouraged any other individual in the exercise or enjoyment of, any right granted or protected by the Act or this part.

c. Illustrations of conduct prohibited by this section include, but are not limited to:

1. Coercing an individual to deny or limit the benefits, services, or advantages to which he or she is entitled under the Act or this part

2. Threatening, intimidating, or interfering with an individual with a disability who is seeking to obtain or use the goods, services, facilities, privileges, advantages, or accommodations of a public accommodation

3. Intimidating or threatening any person because that person is assisting or encouraging an individual or group entitled to claim the rights granted or protected by the Act or this part to exercise those rights

4. Retaliating against any person because that person has participated in any investigation or action to enforce the Act or this part

What You Can Do about It

In addition to federal (and in most cases state) protections from retaliation or coercion in employment, most educators have protections that are outlined in their individual contracts or in the union's negotiated collective bargaining agreement with the district. You can gently remind teachers advocating for your child of this. Teachers should know what their contract says and what it requires of them. They should get a copy of the collective bargaining agreement between their union and their school district. If they have an employee handbook they should read it. In some circumstances, a handbook can help employees form reasonable expectations and impose legal obligations on the teacher's school district.

Teachers who think they're being retaliated against should find out what happened to others who have reached out to the union when they have claimed retaliation or coercion. Does the union have a reputation for standing up to the district, or are they cozy with the administration? If the latter, the teacher may want to consult with a private employment lawyer instead of making the initial contact with the union representative. In addition, parents of kids with disabilities can be good allies. Encourage teachers to reach out to the Special Education PTA (SEPTA or SEPTO) for help.

Proving employment discrimination is not easy. Employers don't put in writing that they are treating an employee a certain way in violation of the law. You're not likely to have a letter that says, "Dear Mrs. Jones, please be informed that we're firing you because you were truthful about the needs of kids with disabilities and we don't want to spend money on them." Retaliation is usually much more subtle than that. Instead, a coercive district will make things very difficult for educators they are trying to discourage. They may suddenly assign all of the children with behavior problems to a teacher's class in one year, then criticize her for how she handled it. Or sometimes educators are suddenly moved to a school that's less desirable, or farther away from their home. Most educators who are being retaliated against know it, but proving it is an entirely different matter. If either teachers or parents are in over their heads, it's a good time to contact a professional.

5

The Tension between Regular and Special Education

What happens when regular educators and special educators don't see eye to eye about a particular child? Tension. We're happy to say that we don't see it often, but when it happens you can cut the tension at an IEP team meeting with a knife. So what's all the fuss about?

We have had many special education teachers tell us about their frustration when regular education teachers do not understand the special education needs of their students. This is understandable when some regular educators do not have more than a cursory understanding of special education. We are sure that many regular educators are dual certified in both regular and special education. We are sure that there are many regular educators who genuinely want to have a better understanding or training and wish that this tension did not exist. But the difference between what regular education teachers and special education teachers learn in school is at the root of some of the tension.

We have also dealt with many regular educators at IEP team meetings who resent the fact that our client's child is in their classroom because they don't believe the child should be participating in the mainstream. These are usually the regular educators who want to leave the IEP team meeting as soon as they have reported how the child is doing in their classroom. This typically happens when the regular education teacher feels little investment in the child due to her minimal participation. It's a shame when this happens.

Regular education teachers asking to leave the meeting early is one of our pet peeves. In most cases, the IDEA mandates that regular education teachers participate in the IEP team meeting. Why? To make sure that the regular education perspective is always considered in team decisions and to ensure that questions that the parents or team have about the general education curriculum can be answered. Consider that the IDEA says, "To the maximum extent appropriate, children with disabilities, including children in public or private institutions or other care facilities, are educated with children who are not disabled, and special classes, separate schooling, or other removal of children with disabilities from the regular educational environment occurs only when the nature or severity of the disability of a child is such that education in regular classes with the use of supplementary aids and services cannot be achieved satisfactorily." Therefore, if a student participates in regular education, even minimally, the role of the regular educator is as important as other perspectives around the table.

Regular education teachers often have special education students who require extra time from them, which in turn causes them added stress in meeting the needs of all of their students. When a regular educator sees that a student is not keeping up with the curriculum or has challenging behaviors, he can refer a student to the team that red-flags students (likely called something like a student assistance team or child study team; find out what it is called in your state). This team then may place the student in Response to Intervention, or RTI (also referred to as Scientific Research-Based Intervention, or SRBI). RTI is a regular education initiative that places struggling students into a three-tiered process of intervention in the hopes that the student will respond to the intervention and get back on track. Sometimes RTI works and sometimes it doesn't. RTI can also be misused and a student who really should be in special education stays in this three-tiered process for way too long, never having been appropriately identified as a student who requires special education.

Let's take a student whose behavior can be disruptive to the classroom. The regular education teacher may want to handle the discipline in a way that is in keeping with her classroom. Meanwhile, the student's IEP calls for a very specific consequence to a specific behavior. The regular education teacher has been instructed through the child's IEP to ignore the student when he taps the desk. The teacher has received training on the plan but simply doesn't like it and refuses to follow it. Every time the student taps the desk, he instructs the student to stop; the student does not stop and the chain of behavior continues. This ends up disrupting the classroom. The regular education teacher reaches out to the special education staff in frustration, which may cause problems for the special educator or school psychologist in charge of overseeing the behavior plan. The special educators request that the teacher follow the "ignoring" aspect of his individualized behavior plan. What's the result? Tension.

As another example, let's consider Susan, an eleventh grader who receives physical therapy in the school pool. Halfway through the school year, the principal told the physical therapist that he could no longer let Susan use the pool because the pool was going to be booked with regular education activities. The PT informed the parent of the change. The parent played "the heavy" and called a meeting with the principal, explaining that she believed her daughter was being discriminated against. She questioned how they could force her to travel to another pool way across town because the regular education activities took precedent over students who need to use the pool for their special education–related services. Susan was allowed to remain in the pool, causing a disruption to the scheduling of the pool. What does this cause between special and regular education? Tension.

Peter has an autism spectrum disorder and is pulled out of class daily to receive discrete trial instruction as a part of the program he is prescribed. This instruction outside of the classroom involves Peter working on specific skills that are broken down into smaller discrete parts, making it easier for him to learn. Peter's parents believe strongly in this programming. His special education team is on board. But his regular education teacher believes that Peter can learn these skills more appropriately in the classroom. What does this disagreement between the teachers cause? Tension.

John is a third grader struggling with writing. His teacher asked the principal to refer him to special education. She was shut down. The principal explained that he couldn't refer one more student to special education for writing because he simply didn't have the resources for it. So the teacher secretly spoke with John's parents and asked them to request an IEP team meeting to refer their son to special education. The parents, relieved that the teacher brought this to their attention, did so. The principal was ticked off and asked the teacher if she knew about the parent's referral. Of course she kept quiet. Do you think this situation caused tension between regular education and special education? Yes.

We don't want to tarnish your image of your school district, and we believe that the examples above represent the exception, not the rule. But we also don't want parents to think that all is rosy when it comes to regular education and special education issues.

What Your School District Isn't Telling You

Your school district is probably not going to tell you that staff on your child's school team are divided, if they are. You might be able to pick up on the tension, but we don't think they will tell you outright about it. If someone does, in all likelihood it will be couched in "this is off the record" kinds of statements. Your school district also won't tell you that there are regular educators who might not like to accommodate, or even refuse to work with, students who have special needs. Some of these people are teachers who have been in the system for years and are nearing retirement; they enjoy the protections of tenure and are not likely to change any time soon. Thankfully, newer regular education teachers have had more exposure and training around the needs of special education students, but that by no means guarantees a smooth process.

We know from experience that in any given school, there may be a stubborn few regular education teachers who do not view students who have IEPs as "their" students, and expect the para educators or special education staff to do all of the heavy lifting. In fairness, this attitude can be exacerbated by special educators who give the regular educators the impression that their involvement in a child's program is merely token. We've read enough pre-IEP meeting emails from special education staff to the child's regular education teacher saying things like, "Can you stop by Tommy's IEP meeting on Thursday for a few minutes to report on progress?" or similar statements that diminish the role of regular educators in the special education process. In other cases, the special education department is desperately trying to get the regular educators to buy in to the kids they serve, with little success.

What You Can Do about It

How can you, as a parent, address this tension? By pointing out the need for ongoing training of staff about a school district's legal obligations to students who have special education needs under the IDEA. If you believe that someone on your team doesn't understand that your child, who has an IEP, is protected under the IDEA, or does not embrace your child as part of the overall school community along with her non-disabled peers, bring this to the attention of your administration, politely and in writing, and request ongoing training. If you've reached this admittedly bad point, you need to document the situation. The letter can go something like this:

> Dear (insert administrator),
>
> A recent situation occurred that led me to understand the divide between some staff members on my

child's, (insert name)'s, IEP team. (Explain here, if appropriate.)

I think it's imperative as we move forward that my son's/daughter's entire team be on the same page as to the understanding of the school district's legal obligations under the IDEA, and disability in general. We are requesting training take place immediately, and be ongoing, within the building among all staff, including both regular and special education. We hope you will consider conducting this training in an effort to reduce tension among my son's/daughter's team and within the building, and to improve the inclusive culture of the school. We believe this can only build a better attitude within the building to be accepting of all children.

Many thanks for your consideration and we look forward to hearing back from you.

(insert your name)

cc: Director of Special Education

6

Other Parents Are Complaining about Your Kid

While we suspect special education administrators might not think we are terribly sympathetic to their jobs, we actually really, truly are. They have a tough job. One of the things that make being the Director of Special Education hard is that you aren't just worrying about one student, as a parent may be; you are responsible for *all* of the students who have disabilities in your district. That sometimes means that one student with disabilities is doing something that impacts another student with disabilities. It may simply be a situation where one student's needs come in direct contrast with another's such that grouping them is problematic. Take, for example, a student who requires the ability to move about the room and to be able to hum being in the same classroom as a student who requires a very quiet, predictable environment in order to focus. At other times the ways in which the competing interests of students with disabilities can manifest themselves can be much more problematic. Physical altercations, bullying, inappropriate sexual interactions—all are examples of the types of situations that arise in our schools and may mean that an administrator must take into account the individual needs, *and the legal rights*, of several students simultaneously. Not easy.

In addition to having to manage all of the needs of the students with IEPs in their district, Special Education Directors also have to manage all of those students' parents. This sometimes means that a director is answering to the parents of one of his students because of the actions of another one of his students. In such circumstances, not only is the director in the middle of these competing issues, but he has to consider each child's needs in the process.

We have had many situations arise with our clients where this is clearly the unenviable position of the administration, and yet the parents (sometimes of each of the students involved) are unaware of the other student. We are sometimes called in to a situation where a student has engaged in inappropriate behavior in school. The district wants to remove the student and place her in another program. The parents believe the student can, with the right support, stay in the program. Often, the parents are shocked that the district wants to remove their child, especially when the district is recommending an outside, costly, private placement as a result. What the parents may not realize is that the parents of the other students in the class may be complaining about their child. A lot. To the administrator. The administrator may even be getting complaints from parents of regular education students. At a certain point, if the question becomes whether to satisfy several irate parents or one, the administrator may decide to remove the one student to appease the other parents.

Another problematic interaction for families occurs when students are bullied. Parents of the victim understandably want to know. "What happened to the bully? Was he expelled? Suspended? What was the discipline meted out to the child who hurt my child?"

Here's the thing: Like it or not, the student who did the bullying has rights, too. Those include the right not to have his disciplinary record broadcast to other parents. Many parents get very angry at the administration for not giving them the information they feel they need to know to determine if justice has been served. But this is one of those situations where what seems fair is not necessarily what the law requires. An administrator in that situation might have to assuage the complaining parents of the victim because he is not permitted to disclose information about another student.

Remember, when dealing with your administration, that your child is one of many whose needs and rights must be considered, and that what may be motivating decisions about your child is concern for other students.

What Your School District Isn't Telling You

You have no legal right to know anything about another student's education, disciplinary record, or other private information that can't be disclosed to third parties (including you) by the school. We would like to think this is a good thing. Can you imagine if someone else had the right to know whatever they wanted to know about your child? Most parents appreciate that their child has a right to privacy in their educational records and information; this is not a right specific to children you happen to love or like. *All* public school children have these protections, regardless of whether or not they have disabilities.

Your administrator may be under a great deal of pressure from you and/or other parents to disclose information about other students, but you should expect them to keep their lips sealed.

What You Can Do about It

If you encounter incidents that involve your child, you can request an incident report. In many states such reports are required to be maintained. However, you may also want more data about the situation, including ABC (Antecedent, Behavior, Consequence) data: antecedent, as in what happened before the incident occurred; behavior, as in what was the behavior of your child; and consequence, as in what happened to your child as a result of her behavior. This should provide you with a good idea of what happened and why it happened to your child.

You are going to have to accept the fact that you may never know what the other child did or if the other child was punished. You need to stay focused on what you and the team can do to identify what made your child vulnerable to the situation and may have caused or contributed to the incident in the first place (though it's possible your kid was just a target, pure and simple). Our clients who are targeted are often being targeted, at least in part, because they lack a social, functional, or adaptive skill. In this case, it's essential to identify what that missing piece is. Once identified, ask yourself, is this lack of skill addressed through my child's IEP? Is there an IEP goal to teach the skill in order to reduce the likelihood that an incident like this will happen again? Are counseling services needed? How can this event help the team address it through the IEP? An objective assessment of the situation may, ultimately, serve to improve your child's program.

7

The Meeting before the Meeting

We live in Connecticut, the land of disparity. One day Julie had an IEP meeting in a wealthy town at 9 am. She drove up to the idyllic, Norman Rockwell–esque school where she saw the principal ringing an old-fashioned school bell and ushering the children into school. Parents walked their children to school from their multimillion-dollar homes on treelined streets in the surrounding neighborhood and kissed their children good-bye at the door. It was a slice of Americana that is not representative of the average town in our country. That afternoon, Julie attended an IEP team meeting at an old, run-down inner-city school with a high-security system.

Some schools hold IEP team meetings in fancy conference rooms with cushy seats and a high-tech phone for conference calls. Other schools are old and in desperate need of an update. But what do all of the IEP team meetings have in common in spite of all of this disparity? They almost never start on time. More often than not, the school staff meets before the official meeting when the parents are invited in. In fact, we are often instructed to sit in the main office and wait to be called in while everyone else on the team is already meeting in the room. Why? When parents are represented by a lawyer or an advocate, it may be for the administrator to calm nerves and make sure the team members are prepared. But more often than not, the reason for the meeting is simple: to strategize without the parents present.

Remember the chapter about money? This is what the meeting before the meeting is typically about. The administrator is usually making sure that whatever decisions get made at the meeting don't exceed the resources of the district.

For example, a parent may be planning to request that her child have three sessions of occupational therapy a week versus the two already provided. The school team knows this will be discussed because the parent has shared her concern with the occupational therapist. The OT lets the administrator know this and might in turn be directed to support the argument on why that extra session will be denied. That explanation can be as simple as stating that the child's program is appropriate with two sessions per week. But why will they really deny the extra session? Here we are back to resources. Some districts do not want to set the precedent of giving one student more services than other similar children. Imagine what would happen if other parents found out. They worry that a slew of parents would call IEP team meetings and demand the same services.

The meeting before the meeting is often when the administrator chairing the meeting meets with the team to understand what is going on and tells the staff around the table what they should and should not say. At its worst, an IEP team meeting is run by the administrator chairing the meeting who doesn't allow staff members to speak unless they are directly asked a question. We've seen administrators say, "OK, let's ask the team what they think. Does anyone think Susie needs extended school year services?" Silence. It's like the scene in *Ferris Bueller's Day Off* when the teacher taking attendance calls Ferris's name. "Bueller? Bueller? Anyone?" Silence.

We spend much of our time reading the body language of participants in IEP team meetings. We've seen staff members look at each other as if to say, "I hope they don't ask me anything." We've also noticed that staff members do not say what you know they would really like to say or what they have told parents in private.

What is the problem with this practice? School districts are not legally entitled to predetermine placement and other IEP team decisions without the parents. What can you do about it? Not much, because proving that a team predetermined a decision without the parents is nearly impossible.

And by the way, if you are ever kept waiting for an unreasonable amount of time while the staff has the meeting before the meeting, ask for the record to reflect your concern that a long meeting took place without you prior to your being invited into the room.

What Your School District Isn't Telling You

Your school administrator most likely will not tell you upon starting your IEP team meeting that, "We all just met and I have told the team what they will say and, more importantly, what they cannot say." If that happens, be sure to document it *immediately*. But it won't. Instead, you have to listen very carefully and be prepared to call team members out when you hear them slip comments into the conversation that make it clear that they've met already.

What You Can Do about It

What can you do about it? This is a tough one. As noted above, proving that a team predetermined a decision without the parents is nearly impossible. Your best bet is to request a copy of all emails among the team discussing your child. Emails that reference your child are part of the educational records to which you are entitled under the Family Educational Rights and Privacy Act (FERPA), and if you suspect the team's been meeting before the IEP meeting to predetermine placement, you may find reference to the meeting in the emails. A request for your child's educational records could go like this:

Dear (insert administrator),

Pursuant to FERPA, I am requesting a copy of all of my child's educational records, including a copy of any and all emails between and among the educators, including administration, referencing or discussing my child, (insert name). Please let me know when I can pick up a set of the records.

Many thanks,

(insert your name)

cc: Director of Special Education

8

The Teacher Needs Help, but Nobody Wants to Say So

We have attended many IEP meetings where it's clear that the problem with the program is clearly identifiable: it's the teacher. And everyone knows it. And nobody wants to say it.

These situations are tough. Most parents we know *hate* the idea of coming off as aggressive toward the team or the teacher, or disparaging the people working with their child. It's the last thing they want to do. But sometimes it's clear that one of the adults on the team is the obstacle to success.

When this happens, we suggest a few things. First, try to gain perspective on the other educators working with the teacher. It's likely that your child is not the only child the other adults are concerned about, and some of the team members may already have complained to or about the teacher internally. They, too, may be frustrated with the situation. Try pulling one of the teachers you know aside outside of the meeting and ask her if there's anything you can do to help.

Next, ask yourself: Are the problems solvable? If given the right support and training, would this person be able to perform the job? Sometimes, a new or inexperienced teacher is given a student whose needs exceed his abilities, or a veteran teacher is asked to work with a student whose disability is not one she has had training to address. Does the teacher seem open to learning, or is he defensive when questioned? If you think his heart is in the right place and you say so, the team may see you as an ally when you ask in the IEP meeting that a consultant be brought in on a regular basis to work with the team or do some training.

If the educator in question is not only unwilling to change, but also wears his ignorance like a badge of honor, handling the situation is much tougher. Parents are not legally entitled to pick which individuals work with their children in their public schools. You can put yourself in a very bad place if you make the administration publicly pick your side or the teacher's side; parents almost always lose that battle.

Getting rid of a particular person on an IEP team is a very hard thing to accomplish, and it's not something you should try to do unless the situation is particularly bad or clearly impacting your child's success. (If this happens to your middle or high schooler, you may be able to solve the problem with one simple schedule change. Drop an elective, switch to a new foreign language, add another hour of study hall, and voila! New teacher!)

What Your School District Isn't Telling You

It is highly unlikely that your school is going to tell you that a staff person is not able to do her job, that she is woefully underqualified or trained, or that "everyone on the team knows she can't do this job." Generally speaking, school administrators protect their staff. Unless a teacher is caught abusing a child on tape, or some other egregious act that supports a collective shaming, chances are administrators are not going to share with parents their concerns about individual educators. On some level, it's understandable. Employers should support their employees, within reason. So, as is often the case, if you learn that a staff member is unqualified, it will either be through your direct knowledge of how they are(n't) doing their job or because another educator told you about it off the record.

What You Can Do about It

When a situation has a harmful impact on your child, it's time to speak up. Start a conversation in a private meeting between you and the administration. Come up with details and facts to back you up. Do not say, "She's not nice to Tommy." Instead, cite concrete examples like, "She told Tommy that he shouldn't be in the reading circle if he can't read aloud, which really upset him." If the person in question is a service provider who is missing service time with your child, keep track! Get as much detail together as possible, and then go in to the administrator with those details.

And while we encourage this meeting to be discreet and private—not in front of the teacher—we still want these concerns documented. So while the meeting may be just between you and the administrator, it should be memorialized by you in an email confirming the discussion and action items. Remember, if it isn't in writing, it didn't happen!

Hopefully the administrator will become motivated to make sure that the situation changes. Give the administrator a chance to do her job. This may include giving the teacher more training and an opportunity to prove himself. It also may mean the administrator needs to document the teacher's failures in order to discipline or terminate him. Be patient, within reason, because these types of changes take time.

9

The Least Trained Person and the Most Complex Children

We are here with some sobering news. Some of the most impaired children in this country are spending most of their day with the least educated professional on the IEP team. Additionally, we often hear that these people—often paras—are banned from speaking directly to parents. We refer to this as the dirty little secret of special education.

We are in schools every day and see things that make us cringe. Some kids who have full-time paras are given tasks like emptying garbage and delivering interschool mail. There may be nothing wrong with this and some parents approve of it if it is part of a transition-to-adulthood program in which this skill is being taught for vocational purposes. But we often see this as time-filling busy work that doesn't seem to develop a skill.

We don't want to sound overly critical. But if a child requires a para, even part-time, he has risen to a higher level of need and all parties should be scrupulously determining the training the paraprofessional needs to provide the child with an appropriate program.

Your state likely has specific guidelines regarding the roles and responsibilities of the para educator. In Connecticut, paraprofessionals are not required to have an advanced degree beyond high school. This means that the week before getting the job, a paraprofessional could have been a stay-at-home mother whose youngest child is finally in school for a full day. Or the para could have been a bank teller. Don't get us wrong. We are both mothers and have nothing against bank tellers. But neither position prepares them to teach the most complex learners in a school.

And even if the paraprofessional has an advanced degree, it could be in accounting, dance, or something totally unrelated to the education of students who have disabilities. And while the paraprofessional may be under the supervision of the certified staff member responsible for the IEP goals, she is still spending the most time with your child during the day. This is why training for the people in these roles is vital to your child's educational success.

We often hear "all of our paras are trained," as if that blanket statement is supposed to instill instant calmness. What does that mean? Trained in what? Trained for how long? Is it a one-shot deal? Is it ongoing? Unfortunately, too often the district's one-size-fits-all approach to training doesn't capture the specific training required to deliver the IEP.

We've seen a situation in which a child had hemophilia and difficulty ambulating and the district refused to provide the para with the training required to keep the child safe. We've seen situations where the child required specific instructional guidelines to be followed and the district refused to provide the para with the prescribed training on the instruction.

For example, there are many types of reading instructions for students with dyslexia and other learning disabilities. Many of the programs that are proven effective require specific training—even certification—in that method. Often, districts will claim a teacher has "training," when in fact they do not have the specific training in the methodology required by the intervention developers. On a more positive note, we've seen districts respond favorably when specific training for the para is requested or recommended by a professional.

Here in Connecticut, legislation was passed that made it mandatory for the paraprofessional to be included around the IEP table if the parents request her presence. Prior to this legislation, parents were routinely denied having the para at the IEP team. Imagine keeping the person least qualified for but most involved in educating your child out of the meeting you depend on to understand your child's program.

What can you do? As a paraprofessional, demand that your district specifically train you if you feel undertrained in any role or responsibility you need to fulfill. As a parent, identify the areas in which your child's paraprofessional requires additional training, how often he should be trained and the reasons for the training, and officially request it through the IEP team meeting process. We feel strongly that training does not ensure competence. It's not a bad idea to request a system that measures the ongoing performance of the para.

What Your School District Isn't Telling You

In all likelihood, your school team won't tell you how your child's para educator or aide is qualified to work with your child unless you ask for that information, and even then, what you learn will be limited. The usual times we have seen administrators provide a great deal of information about a para to a parent is when they have gone out of their way to find someone with exceptional credentials and they want the parents to know about it. Most times, you'll only know the para's first name and if they've ever worked with children with disabilities before.

What You Can Do about It

Check the qualifications your state requires of para educators. In addition, remember that *federal* law provides for the qualifications of such individuals (including the fact that the paraprofessional is not supposed to replace the teacher—only assist her).

Federal law states in pertinent part:

(14) Personnel Qualifications.

a. In General. The State educational agency has established and maintains qualifications to ensure that personnel necessary to carry out this part are appropriately and adequately prepared and trained, including that those personnel have the content knowledge and skills to serve children with disabilities.

b. Related Services Personnel and Paraprofessionals. The qualifications under subparagraph (A) include qualifications for related services personnel and paraprofessionals that

i. are consistent with any State-approved or State-recognized certification, licensing, registration, or other

56

comparable requirements that apply to the professional discipline in which those personnel are providing special education or related services

ii. ensure that related services personnel who deliver services in their discipline or profession meet the requirements of clause (i) and have not had certification or licensure requirements waived on an emergency, temporary, or provisional basis

iii. allow paraprofessionals and assistants who are appropriately trained and supervised, in accordance with State law, regulation, or written policy, in meeting the requirements of this part to be used to assist in the provision of special education and related services under this part to children with disabilities.

c. **Qualifications for Special Education Teachers.** The qualifications described in subparagraph (A) shall ensure that each person employed as a special education teacher in the State who teaches elementary school, middle school, or secondary school is highly qualified by the deadline established in Section 6319(a)(2) of this title.

d. **Policy.** In implementing this section, a State shall adopt a policy that includes a requirement that local educational agencies in the State take measurable steps to recruit, hire, train, and retain highly qualified personnel to provide special education and related services under this part to children with disabilities.

e. **Rule of Construction.** Notwithstanding any other individual right of action that a parent or student may maintain under this part, nothing in this paragraph shall be construed to create a right of action on behalf of an individual student for the failure of a particular State educational agency or local educational agency staff person to be highly qualified, or to prevent a parent from filing a complaint about staff qualifications with the State educational agency as provided for under this part.

In addition, No Child Left Behind has language regarding the training of such personnel. It requires that "All paraprofessionals . . . must have (1) completed two years of study at an institution of higher education; (2) obtained an associate's (or higher) degree; or (3) met a rigorous standard of quality and be able to demonstrate, through a formal State or local academic assessment, knowledge of and the ability to assist in instructing reading, writing, and mathematics."

We want to make sure your child's para educator is trained to implement *your* child's IEP— not all of the IEPs in the school. Ask for your child's IEP to document the specific type of training the para needs, how often it occurs, and who (by discipline, not by name) does the training. If the para doesn't have the necessary training or know-how to implement the training she has received, your child is at risk of spending his entire school day with someone who has no idea how to work with him.

10

Why They Care about Which Label They Give Your Child

Let's start with an explanation of what it means to receive a "label" when your child gets an IEP. Under the IDEA, Congress outlined over a dozen categories of special education eligibility. Many states have their own categories or create variations on the federal disability definitions. When an IEP team, including the parents, decides that a child is eligible for special education and related services, the team is obligated to select which category of disability is listed on the child's IEP as their primary disability. It is entirely separate from a child's diagnosis, which is typically left to outside professionals like pediatricians, psychologists, and psychiatrists.

As a legal matter, which box is checked for the eligibility category is supposed to have no connection to which services a child receives. For example, a district cannot reserve speech services for students whose IEP lists them as a student with a speech or language impairment. Once a child has an IEP, the program must meet the child's unique needs regardless of which label they have been assigned.

For this reason, we have often found ourselves in debates with IEP teams over labels, with the district administration suggesting that, "The label isn't important; she'll get what she needs no matter which category we pick." Well, here's the problem with that. There is such a thing as setting expectations. Whether we want to admit it or not, a student's label creates expectations on the part of the adults as to how the student will learn, behave, and function. Some of those expectations may be good and some may not. Take a student who has an autism spectrum disorder and an emotional disturbance. If you were an educator, would you be prepared for this student if their IEP category were one versus the other? Might you be more forgiving of certain behavior if the student had one category and not the other? When deciding, as a team, which category to pick, these are the types of questions you should be asking. Which category best describes the disability that is interfering with your child's ability to be successful in school?

Your district might have another agenda, one you are not even aware of, when deciding which label to pick. For example, some school districts are being monitored because they have too high, or too low, representation of a particular category of disability in their district. They may not want to issue a particular category to your child simply because they don't want to mess with their numbers. But that shouldn't matter to you; to you, what matters is whether your child is being properly identified.

We have had cases where the argument over label became quite profound. One was a situation where a student had an IEP for many years with the category of a specific learning disability, and after many years of instruction the student's IQ was low enough to qualify for an intellectual disability (ID). The district wanted to change the category to ID in a thinly veiled attempt to suggest that the lack of academic progress was due to the child's innate cognitive limitations, rather than lack of instruction. But the earlier IQ scores were higher, which we felt demonstrated that the issue was the failure to remediate the learning disability, resulting in a decline in cognitive functioning in the testing. That debate ended up in court. So, yes, labels can matter.

If your district recommends an eligibility category with which you disagree, remember that you have the right to disagree with the category just as you have a right to disagree with proposed services. If you are asked why the category matters, since the label won't be tied to programming, remind the team that the IDEA requires that a label be picked; there must be a reason for that requirement, and one of them is to make sure that we properly identify which disability causes the child to require special education services.

Finally, while in many cases what looks like one disability when a child is six can look very different when a child is nine and then twelve, you should be wary if your child is given a different label every time her eligibility is reconsidered. When we see files that indicate that a child's eligibility category keeps changing, we know that it's time for a good, Independent Educational Evaluation.

What Your School District Isn't Telling You

They probably won't tell you if they are being monitored because of the number of students with a particular label in their district. To sum it up, they won't tell you why they may be motivated to choose a specific label over another.

It's important to say a word here about state labels. The federal law *does* allow states to create their own labels, and there are some that are far more helpful than those created by the IDEA. However, remember that federal law takes precedence in most cases. So if your child qualifies for special education services under federal law, your school district can't deny them eligibility simply because he doesn't meet a state-created label.

Most states maintain a guideline and checklist for each label that may assist you in answering the questions of whether your child meets criteria for eligibility.

What You Can Do about It

If your child has a diagnosis that you have obtained on your own, provide it to the team and ask to go over your state's guidelines of eligibility for the disability that most aligns with the diagnosis. Remember, you can have a medical diagnosis and not have the disability rise to the level of requiring an IEP for specialized instruction.

In the event that your team refuses to consider reviewing the guidelines based on the diagnosis that you have provided to them, request an Independent Educational Evaluation (IEE) in the area of suspected disability. If they grant you an IEE, great! Ask for the district's IEE guidelines, do your research, and choose an evaluator who has a good reputation among parents. Remember that an assessment isn't worth the paper it is written on if it doesn't answer your diagnostic and programming questions. ("Diagnostic" means what is your child's diagnosis? How does it impact him in school and his learning of academic, functional, and adaptive skills? And should your child be found eligible for special education services? "Programming" means what specific interventions must be in place to appropriately meet your child's special education needs?) The more specificity the better!

If the district refuses your request for an IEE, it must file for a due process hearing to defend its evaluation, without delay. Read the procedural safeguards the district has provided you and refer to chapter 14, which covers IEEs. Whether you obtain an IEE at public expense or get one on your own, once complete, present the findings to the IEP team. Eligibility, including which label, should be discussed and decided. Remember, just as with all decisions that the IEP team makes, you have a right to disagree with the label your team recommends, and to exercise your right to ask that it be changed.

11

The Perils of Doing Nothing: Lessons from Sandy Hook

As two special education professionals from Connecticut, it's impossible to ignore the tragedy at Sandy Hook. We would be remiss not to include it in this book. We are not discussing it here to be sensational. We are not including it to shine a light on who is to blame, as there were several factors that led to this tragedy. What the public largely does not know, but we know, as do parent attorneys and advocates throughout the nation, is that numerous violations of the IDEA underpinned the series of events that culminated in the massacre of elementary school children and educators in Newtown. Indeed, this position has been painstakingly documented by the State of Connecticut's Office of the Child Advocate (OCA), a state agency, in a report dated November 21, 2014.

The report states that the role that educational and health-care systems played in Adam Lanza's deterioration is not entirely clear, and that "[n]o direct line of causation can be drawn from these to the horrific mass murder at Sandy Hook." However, the facts are impossible for us to ignore.

We want to state at the outset, and in unequivocal terms, that autism spectrum disorders, mental health challenges, and emotional disorders do not predispose people to be violent. In fact, the opposite is true. Recent research reveals that most violent people do not suffer from mental illness, and that people with mental disorders are significantly more likely to be victims of violent crime, not perpetrators. In fact, studies have shown that people with severe mental illness are over two times more likely to be attacked, raped, or mugged than the general population. People with Asperger syndrome are no more likely than the general population to commit a crime; those with "classic autism" are less likely than other people to commit crimes.

What *is* true is that many students with particular emotional or behavioral disabilities require explicit, reliable, consistent intervention to develop and maintain appropriate social, coping, functional, and adaptive skills. The IDEA requires this. It's one of the major reasons that school districts have an obligation to identify students who have disabilities and evaluate them. Every professional advocate and attorney who represents children has cases where the student's emotional state deteriorates so much that the child could be a danger to himself or others. We see it often. When Sandy Hook happened, we worried that time would reveal that Adam Lanza was such a student.

Never before have we so hated being right.

The OCA report documents repeated, consistent, blatant violations of the IDEA by the Newtown Public Schools. Adam moved to Newtown with his parents and attended first grade at Sandy Hook Elementary School. He arrived with an IEP from his preschool in New Hampshire, where his eligibility category

66

was "Speech or Language Impaired." It does not appear Newtown conducted its own evaluation. In first grade he received thirty minutes each of speech and occupational therapy services per week. By second grade, the OT services were discontinued. By third grade, he was only receiving a total of thirty minutes weekly of speech articulation therapy. Newtown Public Schools "exited" Adam from special education services entirely by the fourth grade. In response, Adam's mother wrote the school asking for consideration in teacher assignment for fifth grade, noting Adam's tendency for anxiety and depression.

In fifth grade, ten-year-old Adam and another student co-authored "The Big Book of Granny" for a school project. The book references cannibalism and child murder. According to the OCA: "While many children, and especially boys, of this age contend with anger and violent impulses in their play and creative productions, 'The Big Book of Granny' stands out, *to mental health professionals,* as a text marked by extreme thoughts of violence that should have signified a need for intervention and evaluation." No IEP referral was made, though it appears the Newtown administration was aware of the book, as they "spoke to" Adam because he was trying to sell copies for a quarter. The OCA found that, by this point, just one year after being exited from special education services, "the need for a comprehensive diagnostic evaluation performed by a licensed specialist is evident."

By sixth grade, Adam became more anxious and unhappy, with OCD symptoms, including excessive hand washing. He began experiencing panic attacks at school. A parent in the neighborhood later described him during this time, according to the OCA report: "[He was] not connecting with anyone at all. . . . He was not bullied, however, he was just left alone. . . . He never associated with others and when he got on the bus he would sit with his headphones and listen to music. [My daughter] tried to be nice by saying hi, but Adam would not make eye contact with others." The only plan in place was to have his mother pick him up from school when he would become overwhelmed by his anxiety.

According to the OCA, "Adam attended Newtown Middle School for grade 7. It was during Grade 7 that his social, emotional, and communicative struggles appeared to have become increasingly intense, culminating in his abrupt withdrawal from the Newtown Middle School at the end of the third quarter, in late April 2005. There is no indication in the record that he was offered a re-evaluation for special education services based on social-emotional or other developmental concerns." In the last quarter of seventh grade, he attended a Catholic school. In the OCA report his teacher there noted, "[A]fter my years of experience teaching 7th-grade boys, I know how they are supposed to act. But I saw AL as being not normal with very distinct antisocial issues. AL was a very intelligent boy but he was also very quiet, barely spoke, and never responded to his classmates' kindness of trying to help him fit in." Adam continued his extremely violent writing in school. He abruptly withdrew at the end of the school year from the Catholic school.

Adam did not attend any school for eighth grade, remaining home with his mother for the year. He was not homeschooled, but rather received homebound tutoring services (starting in December) from the Newtown Public Schools. These are entirely different things. Homeschooling is when a parent chooses to educate their own child at home; homebound tutoring is a service provided by a school district to a child at home. Putting Adam on such an isolating and restrictive plan as homebound tutoring with no therapeutic support, further marginalizing him and his mother from the typical school community, was likely one of Newtown's biggest mistakes.

Adam's mother brought him to the ER for crisis intervention in September of his eighth grade year. At that time he was five eight and weighed ninety-eight pounds. Hospital records described him as "anxious," "withdrawn," and "hesitant to be touched." He presented as agitated, hypervigilant, and overwhelmed with fear. The clinical consultation resulted in diagnoses of Anxiety Disorder, Not Otherwise Specified, followed by a discharge diagnosis of Asperger syndrome and obsessive compulsive disorder. After the ER visit, Adam began seeing a local psychiatrist, whose name his mother obtained from the Newtown Public Schools.

A December IEP meeting was finally held when Adam was in eighth grade, the first time the Newtown team considered Adam's special needs since he was exited in fourth grade. The IEP approved ten hours per week of homebound tutoring through the IEP, with potential evaluators meeting with him to establish rapport. A second IEP meeting held in June of eighth grade indicated that "AL's primary disability was 'to be determined,' but the team agreed to defer evaluation due to his extreme anxiety and the psychiatrist's recommendations. A schedule of courses was listed for his possible 9th grade entry into Newtown High School." The OCA report notes: "What response could the school system have had, and what was its capacity to screen and evaluate AL in all areas of suspected disability, as required by state and federal law? The school district appears to have accepted the recommendations of the mother and the community psychiatrist for homebound place-ment (without instruction) with no documented discussion of alternatives. It is difficult to determine why there was no review of therapeutic school settings as a consideration for placement or even other therapeutic supports that could be put in place for AL in the school setting. Additionally, there was very little scrutiny of AL's homebound placement."

While it appears that at times during eighth grade Adam's parents refused educational services (by not sending him to school), *at no time* was the Department of Children and Fami-lies contacted by the mandated reporters in the school, nor was Adam or his family referred for truancy charges.

Between eighth and ninth grades, after the Lanzas divorced, Adam's father took him to Yale for an evaluation. The Yale Child Study Evaluation Team recommended imme-diate and intensive therapeutic intervention. According to the team: "AL's mother told the Yale psychiatrist that he used to look at people but did not anymore. AL then asked rhetori-cally, 'Why should I have to.' When the doctor explained all of the information that a person could learn by looking at a facial expression, such as a smile, AL stated that people could interpret smiles differently: 'Some primates smile when they are frightened.' When asked for three magic wishes, AL could not think of any and instead he said that 'he would wish that whatever was granting the wishes would not exist.'"

The Yale team noted: "*Beyond the impact of OCD symp-toms on himself and his mother, we are very concerned about AL's increasingly constricted social and educational world....* Inability to tolerate even minimal interaction with even older more mature classmates will have grave consequences for his future education and social and occupational adaptation unless means of remediation are found. Inability to interact with classmates will prove increasingly deleterious to education. *We believe it is very important to reframe the discussion with school from issues of curricular content to much more urgent issues of how to accommodate AL's severe social disabilities in a way that would permit him to be around peers and to progress, rather than regress, socially, as well as academically.*"

Both parents asked for changes to the IEP as a result of the Yale recommendations. Newtown did not change his program. Adam attended Newtown High School intermittently, receiving homebound tutoring on occasion through the district. He continued to be socially withdrawn, and informed the district at the start of eleventh grade that he wanted to finish high school early. The school district willingly accelerated him through his credits, giving him a diploma *a year early*, thereby terminating his special education services and what little thread remained between him and societal norms.

What Your School District Isn't Telling You

Several factors, including more than one system of care, failed at Sandy Hook. We are not suggesting that the Newtown Public Schools are solely to blame. However, the record is clear, and not disputed, that the district did not meet its obligations to identify Adam as a student who required intensive therapeutic support. And why? The same reason we've identified throughout this book: these services are expensive.

What You Can Do about It

All we can do is hope to learn from this horrible tragedy. Our lessons:

1. Public schools are the first responders, under the IDEA, for children with emotional and behavioral disabilities.
2. Public schools have the affirmative legal duty to identify children with emotional disabilities.
3. Public schools have the duty to provide services to children whose disabilities are emotional, social, or behavioral, not just academic.
4. Public schools need to treat parents as allies, not as enemies, and to offer assistance or notify the authorities if parents are unable or unwilling to meet their child's needs.
5. Special education administrators should work in concert with families and advocates to ensure that training on identifying students with disabilities occurs not just for special educators, but for regular education providers as well.

Part 2: Moving Forward

Parents who take on their school districts often feel like they are in a David versus Goliath battle. This is especially hard for most parents to wage, when many are already physically, emotionally, and financially tapped by the challenges they face raising a child, or children, with disabilities. Given how large the population of students with special education needs is (approximately 15 percent of the overall population of students), these parents should be strong, organized, and powerful. Some are. They are the ones who figured out what their legal rights were, and learned how to enforce them. We want these parents to be the norm, not the exception. We want parents to learn from our years of experience, so they can start applying these skills today, not when their child is about to age out of services and the parent finally figures out the system.

We've shown how special education decisions can be corrupted by money and power. Now is the time to learn your rights and apply them to help your child succeed in school and beyond. Use your knowledge as power.

12

You Have Rights

You *do* have rights. As the parent of a child who has a disability or disabilities, you have rights, and your child has rights. Lots and lots of rights!

There are several federal laws that govern schoolchildren with disabilities that every public school in the country (and yes, that means charter and magnet schools too) has to follow. You might need to use several of them over time, but for purposes of this book, and for the most efficient use of your time, you need to learn about two of them: Section 504 and the Individuals with Disabilities Education Act (IDEA).

Section 504 of the Rehabilitation Act of 1973 (usually just referred to as "504" or "Section 504") has several components, including antiretaliation and antidiscrimination provisions protecting individuals with disabilities, and those who advocate for them. In addition, Section 504 provides that public schools (because they are entities that receive federal funding) cannot discriminate against students with disabilities in school, and therefore must provide reasonable accommodations to them so that they can learn like their nondisabled peers. Section 504 is triggered for students whose disabilities need accommodations in school, rather than specialized instruction. An easy example is a child with a serious food allergy. That child doesn't need to be taught differently, but he may very well need accommodations in the lunch room or elsewhere in the school building to be sure he can access his education. That child would likely get a 504 Plan. A tougher example is a child with attention deficit hyperactivity disorder (ADHD). Some kids who have ADHD might need only preferential seating, to take more breaks during class, or have extra time on tests. These students may be well served with only a 504 accommodations plan. But some students with ADHD require specialized instruction in order to benefit from their education; accommodations alone are not enough, and they may need actual services.

This is where the distinction between 504 and the IDEA becomes easier to see. Section 504 is largely an accommodations act. The IDEA, on the other hand, is a services act, and students who qualify for services under the IDEA get Individualized Education Programs (IEPs), rather than accommodation plans (though IEPs include accommodations and modifications as well). Every public school in every state and territory in the United States of America has to follow the IDEA. They receive federal funding to do so. They don't receive enough federal funding, but the IDEA is a partially funded mandate, not an unfunded mandate.

It is, however, a *mandate*—as is Section 504. They are not optional, discretionary, or otherwise subject to the whims or moods of your school district.

We know, however, that sometimes it doesn't feel that way. It seems like the system is totally stacked against parents! If your school district isn't giving your child what she needs, or you suspect it isn't, how can you get what your child needs? Here's the answer: *you* have to enforce your rights. That's right, you do, as a parent. The federal and state governments provide some oversight, but they are not enforcing your child's individual rights.

The government might at some point make a school district or state change a policy or practice, but that doesn't help your daughter learn how to read or your son learn how to speak. The sad truth is that parents of children with disabilities are forced to become private attorneys general. They have to enforce the federal laws that protect their children.

The good news is that parents don't have to lawyer up or bring in a professional advocate in order to get what they are entitled to under the IDEA and 504. What you need is to know how to enforce those rights on your own. Why? Because if you learn how to apply the laws that are designed to help you and your child, your child is far more likely to end up with the skills he needs to be successful in life. And that's what it's all about: outcomes.

Are you ready to be empowered? Excellent! Here's how we're going to empower you. First, we're going to give you the most important rights you need to know about. There are dozens and dozens of procedural and other requirements under the IDEA and 504, but you don't need to know each and every one of them. The most important ones are the ones that usually make the difference between a quality educational program and a substandard one—or worse, a program that looks like a quality program on paper but in reality is not.

What Your School District Isn't Telling You

Although your district may keep a lot of information from you, in this case it *will* tell you that you have rights, because it's

77

required to do so. What it likely *won't* do is anything to make sure you understand them. And while it is required to provide you with the IDEA's procedural safeguards (rules the district has to follow), most often the receipt of these rights becomes a perfunctory part of the IEP team meeting, with little effort to explain what all of the language means. Every state differs in how it complies with this portion of the federal law. But we know this for sure: no matter how your rights are presented to you in writing, they are overwhelming! We have many clients who are attorneys and they have admitted that they have never read them, and if they have, they don't really understand them. Why? Most law schools don't offer a special education law course, and if they do, it's not required. It's a niche area of the law. And it's complicated.

What You Can Do about It

Even if you hate it, read your procedural safeguards. If you don't understand them, read them. Then read them again. Some of it will start to sink in. Compile your questions about them. You are a parent, and you have a child who has special education needs. You can't sit back and hope that all of the professionals are doing the right thing. If you want to optimize the outcome of your child's functioning across all domains—academically, behaviorally, socially, emotionally, and adaptively—you have to step up to the plate and educate yourself. Don't accept the status quo. You're a vital member of your child's IEP team, recognized by the IDEA as a necessary player. Capitalize on the fact that you are entitled to parent training as a related service and ask for it. Capitalize on the fact that you are a valued member of the team and understand your child's IEP, how he's being taught, and whether progress is happening. Simply put, you *must* understand your rights under the IDEA and how your state's IEP paperwork is laid out, or your child's education will be in jeopardy. Period. You're not going to learn all of this overnight. Take one bite of the apple at a time. But don't give up!

13

The Right to Ask for an Evaluation for Services

To channel Maria von Trapp: "Let's start at the very beginning." What if your child isn't identified for services? You suspect your child has a disability, or perhaps someone (your pediatrician or an outside therapist or psychologist) has already issued a diagnosis. What do you do to make sure your child gets the help she needs in school?

First and foremost, know this: you do *not* have to wait for your school to decide if it also sees the difficulties your child is having. In fact, it often doesn't, or your child's teacher is so busy handling her other commitments and obligations in the classroom that she isn't able to focus on your child exclusively. Also, parents have years of experience with their children, whereas teachers might attribute a child's performance or behavior to settling in to a new school year or typical of kids that age. But we have learned one very important lesson over the decades that we have been waging legal battles with school districts: parents have good instincts. So if your gut is telling you something isn't right, something probably isn't right. Congress recognized this, which is why you, as a parent, have an absolute right to ask that your child be evaluated for special education.

What does this mean? It's important to look at it as a process: a child is not automatically given services. The process outlined by law is that a school district must first evaluate the child to determine if he needs services. Then the results of those evaluations are reviewed by the IEP team. Next, the team, including the parents, determines if the child meets criteria for services and/or accommodations. Then the team, including the parents, determines what that service or accommodation plan might be. Referring your child to special education or asking your school district to evaluate your child to determine if she is eligible for services may be the first step. It means you are asking for a determination of whether your child needs an IEP or a 504 Plan. Many times, teachers or other educators will refer a child to the IEP team to consider if he is eligible. However, this does not mean that only educators can make the referral; you can as the parent, and it's an absolute right you have by federal law.

Your child's teacher may ask you to make the referral to special education. Why would that happen if a teacher can also, by law, ask that a child be evaluated for services? Because of the pressure teachers sometimes get from school administrators. Remember that your school is a governmental agency. Let us say that again: your public school is a governmental agency. They have a budget, and they have to allocate that budget to a number of competing interests. Special education services can be costly to provide. So when a teacher decides to refer a child in her classroom for an evaluation for special education services, she is taking the first step toward a potentially large financial commitment on behalf of their employer. It should not shock you, therefore, that administrators in some schools very clearly tell teachers *not* to refer students for special education evaluations.

Is that lawful? No. Does it happen every day? Yes. So as a result, parents often tell us that their child's teacher expresses concern about how their child is developing, but says the parents should ask for the meeting. In that circumstance, absolutely request the meeting, but document who told you to make the request, when, and where. You might need it one day.

When can you refer your child for special education evaluation? At any time in his education. Your pediatrician can refer your child as an infant or toddler to early intervention services (known as "Birth to Three" or "Birth to Five" services in many states), but you can too. Your child's teacher can refer her for testing by the school team, but you can too, at any time from when your child enters school until she graduates from high school. You can request this even if your child previously received a 504 Plan or IEP and then was "exited" from that support. If your child is receiving other types of support (such as Response to Intervention or RTI, "tier one," "tier two," or some other such label), you still have the right to ask that your child be evaluated for special education services. It is your right under law, and if you are concerned about your child's education, then you should exercise that right.

Also keep this in mind: education encompasses way more than just academics. Education includes social, functional, behavioral, and adaptive skills. If your kid is a whiz at reading but can't hold a conversation with a peer, that is educational.

If your child gets straight As when she attends school but has been in and out of psychiatric hospitals for most of the year due to depression and anxiety, that is clearly impacting her education because she has not been attending school. These categories are rarely as neat and tidy as you might think.

Your school might require you to complete a form if you want to make the referral for a special education evaluation. That's okay, as long as they don't use the form to delay holding the meeting, conducting the evaluation, or considering your request. If your child's teacher, principal, or other educator tells you that you need to fill out a form to ask for a special education meeting, ask him for the form. This, too, should be documented. If he doesn't send it, ask again. Keep asking and document your requests until you get that form. Once you get it, fill it out, keep a copy, send it in, and stay on top of the scheduling of the meeting. Remember: nobody is in line behind you to advocate for your child.

What Your School District Isn't Telling You

This one is pretty straightforward. your school district doesn't necessarily want you to know that you, as the parent, have a right to ask that your child be evaluated by your school district. The fact that your school team members may not think your child needs evaluating is not the point. They can decide if they want to refer him for an evaluation; but it's up to you to decide if you want to. So don't fall for the line we usually hear: "Let's ask the team if they think an evaluation is necessary." That's irrelevant; the request for the evaluation is coming from the parent, who has the right to make it.

What You Can Do about It

Because your right to have your district evaluate your child is so clear, thankfully, this is one of the things that you can do something about. If you ask your school to evaluate your child and they refuse, it's time to call your state Department of Education and consider filing a complaint (see chapter 3 to learn how).

14

The Right to a Second Opinion

Your district must evaluate your child "in all suspected areas of disability," according to the IDEA. Further, this type of thorough evaluation must occur at least every three years (referred to as a "triennial"), although evaluations can be undertaken more frequently if requested or needed. If your child has been evaluated by your school district, you may not think that the testing is accurate or the result is a fair description of your child's strengths, weaknesses, or educational needs. This may occur during an initial evaluation (when you are first determining if your child is eligible for special education services) or after a reevaluation many years into the process.

So what do you do if you disagree with some or all of the school's testing? Consider using one of the most powerful tools in a parent's special education toolbox: the right to an Independent Educational Evaluation, or IEE. The IEE is, essentially, your right as a parent to obtain a second opinion about your child from an outside evaluator who is paid by the school district, but chosen by you.

The law surrounding IEEs is highly complex, and there are few aspects of special education litigation fraught with more confusion than this one. For example, school administrators will often ask parents why they disagree with the school district's evaluation or evaluations. Parents are not required by law to answer this question, and for good reason. Congress, when developing the IDEA, recognized the fact that parents are not usually educators who understand all of the complexities of the assessments, and are not able to articulate why they disagree. We've heard of situations where schools have told parents that they will not grant the IEE unless the parents can explain why they disagree with the evaluation. This is not a hoop you have to jump through, by law.

School district evaluations often do not include prescriptive recommendations regarding specifics of programming—the road map for how to proceed. So when securing an IEE, make sure you request that the evaluator's assessment includes an observation in school. This allows the evaluator to see firsthand how your child is functioning in school. This observation does not have to be confined to the classroom; it can include any other aspect of the day that the evaluator, or you, thinks is important to see. Some independent evaluators do not conduct school observations and are still excellent evaluators, but a school evaluation is ideal. You might also want to consider submitting parent diagnostic and/or programming questions. You want to make sure that the Independent Educational Evaluation you finally obtain addresses your specific questions about diagnosis and programming. If you don't ask specific questions, the evaluation may not address your area of concern and what to do about it. Finally, ask that the evaluator attend the IEP meeting that reviews the evaluation in person or, at the very least, by phone. The team does not have to agree to this request, but we certainly think it makes sense to have the person who wrote the evaluation there to answer questions from the team, including the parents.

An IEE at district expense must be performed by a person who is *not* an employee of your school district—so avoid the "We can have the speech pathologist from the high school readminister the testing" approach. However, just because someone isn't an employee of the district does not mean that they are unbiased. There are many, many private evaluators out there who make their living from evaluations paid for by school districts, and they do not want to alienate school districts by recommending services that are costly. Your goal is to get an evaluation by someone who does not have a vested interest in the outcome of the evaluation, and that excludes all district personnel and many private evaluators who are regular consultants to school districts.

It's essential that you ask around, especially among other parents of children with disabilities, support groups, parent advocates and attorneys, and other resources to find out whether the evaluator/s you want your district to fund are truly independent. To that end, while districts should and do maintain lists of evaluators who meet their criteria to perform IEEs, you are not restricted to that list; indeed, many parent advocates would argue that this is the list of the people you should avoid! If your district gives you their list, ask it to also provide to you, in writing, the criteria it uses for IEEs. The law states that the district can't use different criteria for evaluations it obtains and evaluations requested by parents. You'll want that criteria to determine that it's not overly burdensome, thereby insuring that you won't be able to get a truly unbiased second opinion; if it is, that criteria may well be illegal and impermissible. Remember, it's called an *Independent* Educational Evaluation for a reason.

You might agree with some of the district's evaluations but not others. If so, ask for the IEE in the discipline or area you disagree with. For example, you might agree that the district's occupational therapy evaluation is appropriate but not agree with the psychological evaluation. In that case, you can simply ask for the psychological IEE. As a general rule, your right to ask for an IEE is limited to one evaluation per discipline for each evaluation the district performs.

Your district does not have to agree to perform the IEE. However, if it doesn't agree, it must, without delay, file for a due process hearing at which it must prove to a hearing officer that the evaluation/s it performed are appropriate. If the hearing officer disagrees, he may order the district to fund the IEE with the evaluator of your choice. (Note that if you are at the hearing level over an IEE, you should have at least consulted with counsel.)

Another important consideration when contemplating an IEE at district expense is whether the type of evaluation you are looking for is a type the district has never performed on your child. If, for example, you suspect your child has an emotional disturbance and your district has never performed a psychiatric evaluation, do you need to first have your school conduct a psychiatric evaluation, and then disagree with it and ask for the IEE? Probably not. If you disagree with your district's testing because it wasn't comprehensive enough, you can ask for the IEE to fill in the gaps in the district's testing.

Technically, any evaluation performed by a person who is not an employee is an independent evaluation, including private testing obtained by parents. If parents obtain their own IEE at their own expense, they can share it with their school team, and by law, the team *must* consider the information contained in the report. Some families choose to go this route rather than getting into a debate with their school district about an IEE at public expense, but remember that your district might not take an outside evaluation like this as seriously as one they fund at public expense.

Parents can always seek to have their private evaluation reimbursed by the district as well, even after they have obtained it.

Why are IEEs so important? Because you can't know what intervention to provide, what a child's program should look like, and whether the services and accommodations are appropriate unless you have a thorough, comprehensive, and unbiased assessment of your child. Can school district staff perform excellent evaluations? Of course, and many of them do. But remember, the recommendations made in evaluations conducted by school personnel are, by definition, employees putting in writing recommendations that might cost their employer money—in some cases, a whole lot of money. Not all educators feel comfortable doing that. In addition, there are some disabilities that, due to their complexity, or because they are extremely rare, require an expertise that is not often found in a public school–based team. For these reasons, make sure that your request for an IEE doesn't come across as a personal affront, but confidently conveys your request for a second opinion. Be prepared: the IEE request often sends school teams into defensive mode. Don't let the team's reaction dissuade you from getting a true picture of your child's educational needs.

Since the IDEA does not require that IEE requests be made at an IEP team meeting, you can request an IEE of your district separately, in writing. Consider writing to your child's administrator, case manager, or whoever chairs her IEP meetings, as follows:

> Dear (insert administrator):
>
> I disagree with the evaluation that the school has performed on my child, (insert child's name and date of birth). I am requesting an Independent Educational Evaluation at public expense in (insert area you want tested). Please let me know whether the district will be agreeing to this IEE, and if so, please send me the district's criteria for independent evaluators. If not, please be sure that I am notified when the district files for a due process hearing without delay to defend its own evaluation.
>
> Many thanks,
>
> (insert your name)
>
> cc: Director of Special Education

What Your School District Isn't Telling You

Let's put it this way: we don't recall many times when a school district reminded parents that they had the right to disagree with their district evaluations and suggest they obtain an

Independent Educational Evaluation at district expense. It's one of the most important rights you have. It costs the district hundreds, if not thousands, of dollars, and it's a well-kept secret in many schools.

What You Can Do about It

You can't get away with not understanding this protection. It is essential to your child's future. The district is obligated to identify every child with a disability in the district, even if he doesn't attend the public schools and never has. It has an obligation to determine if a child requires special education services. If so, the district must offer them. If services are accepted, the district must make sure that the services are provided and that the child receives a free and appropriate public education. Every year. Possibly through high school or early adulthood. And where did the process begin? With an evaluation! If you are concerned, exercise your right to an independent evaluation so that your child doesn't lose years of needed, specialized instruction.

15

Counseling and Training Are Not Just for Kids

Parenting is incredibly hard. Kids don't come with a manual, and there's a reason most people say that being a parent is the hardest thing they have ever done in their lives. This includes parents who have climbed mountains, performed brain surgery, and sent rockets into space. Tina Fey said her greatest life accomplishment is that her children say "please" and "thank you." And she's Tina Fey!

Parenting a child, or children, with disabilities can be a whole other challenge. Most parents don't have degrees in child development, education, special education, behavior, psychology, speech pathology, psychiatry, or the law. Even those who do have hired us to represent their children because it's impossible to be objective and unemotional about your own child. Add to that the educational and legal terminology that comes with advocating for your child's special education needs, and you can see why many parents are so frustrated.

Here's where the least utilized related service under the IDEA comes in handy: parent counseling and training. Federal law authorizes school districts to provide assistance to parents to help them understand their child's disability and child development and to help them acquire the skills necessary to support their child's special education program.

There are many different types of parent training, depending on the parent's needs. The training might focus on how to use technology that the school team uses with her child to assist in communication. It might give a parent behavioral strategies to support her child's program. Or it may involve consultants coming into the home to teach daily living skills. There are countless ways that parent counseling and training can happen. Unfortunately, it doesn't happen nearly enough.

We very rarely see districts incorporate parent counseling and training into a student's IEP, even when it's clear that the family desperately needs this support. Also, some districts like to lump parent training into school-wide assemblies or lectures on disability. While we think providing information to parents like this is a great idea, the information is hardly individualized enough to help a parent understand his child's unique needs. Further, putting group parent training together puts a family in the unenviable, and questionably legal, position of not being able to ask questions about their child without disclosing her disability to other parents.

Some parents bristle at the term "parent training," as it conveys the impression that the parent doesn't know how to parent. We don't disagree; it's one of many terms in the law that we don't think are well named. However, we discourage parents from dismissing the service just because of the label. Think of it this way: it's more training in the IEP than it is training in being a parent.

There are other services that can be incorporated into an IEP, but many are covered in other books that cite the IDEA chapter and verse. We are highlighting parent counseling and training here because it is so underutilized. As you know, your child's disability doesn't go into hibernation at the end of the school day!

What Your School District Isn't Telling You

In our opinion, parent counseling and training is the least known and most underutilized related service under the IDEA. Your school district probably won't go out of its way to tell you the purpose of parent counseling and training (to help parents acquire skills in order to support the implementation of the IEP) and what it can entail; in fact, many educators don't know about this related service themselves.

Parent counseling and training:

- Helps parents understand the educational needs of their child
- Provides parents with information about child development
- Provides support and basic information about a child's initial placement in special education
- Provides parents with contact information about parent support groups, financial assistance resources, and other potential sources of information or support outside the school system

Parents also learn:

- A better understanding of their child's disability
- Ways to be an equal team member
- A better understanding of future implications for their child
- Ways to discuss the disability with their child
- How to be active participants in developing and implementing IEP goals and objectives
- How to use assistive technology devices if they are a part of their child's program
- Ways to help other parents who have children with the same disability

What You Can Do about It

Simple: ask for it. If you feel you need training in order to support your child's IEP, ask your IEP team for parent training. Be prepared to articulate why you are asking for it and what form you want it to take, and be able to defend your position. Do your research and ask for specific training programs or services. For example, if you know a conference is coming up in your state about understanding the IEP or your child's specific disability, provide your district with the details: give administrators a brochure, flyer, or link to the conference. Ask for this training at the IEP team meeting or put your request in writing and ask for a written response. Your email might go like this:

Dear (insert administrator),

I have taken a great interest in understanding my child's disability and in acquiring the skills to support the implementation of her Individualized Education Program (IEP). In my ongoing effort to gain the skills needed to support my child's IEP, I am requesting parent counseling and training in (insert area listed).

I am requesting to attend (insert specific training listed) on (insert date) at (insert location). Attached is information about the program.

I want to thank you for considering my request and look forward to hearing from you in writing. Should you deny my request, please support in writing the specific reason(s) why you will be denying it.

Many thanks,

(insert your name)

cc: Director of Special Education

Parent training will help you, your child, and the district move forward with your child's IEP.

16

Discrimination, Retaliation, Intimidation, Oh My!

Add to this chapter title the word *coercion*; it didn't fit nicely into our chapter title. One of the unfortunate realities of the special education system is that some school district people can become incredibly angry when parents exercise their rights. This is particularly true if you have an overly zealous administrator. At other times the school building or schedule is set up in a way that results in discrimination against children with disabilities, even though the discrimination is not intentional. This can result in parents of children with special education needs being treated in extremely unfair ways. We're here to tell you that it's not just unfair; it's illegal.

Section 504 of the Rehabilitation Act, which we referenced in chapter 1, is not just a law that allows students with disabilities to receive reasonable accommodations in school. It is also an antidiscrimination law. It states that students with disabilities cannot be discriminated against by school districts. School districts receive federal funding and therefore cannot discriminate against those with disabilities as a matter of federal law, which states: "No otherwise qualified individual with a disability in the United States shall, solely by reason of her or his disability, be excluded from the participation in, denied the benefits of, or be subjected to discrimination under any program or activity receiving Federal financial assistance . . ."

Section 504 also covers people who advocate on behalf of students with disabilities, including a child's parents. You know who else enjoys the protections of Section 504 and can't be retaliated against for speaking out on behalf of students with disabilities? Teachers. Teachers cannot be demoted, transferred, fired, or otherwise retaliated against for advocating for students with disabilities. Indeed, many teachers have successfully sued their employers for retaliating against them because they advocated for more intensive programming for children in their schools. Section 504 is overseen by the United States Department of Education's Office for Civil Rights, also known as OCR. OCR complaints can be filed online by any person who believes he has been discriminated against on the basis of disability.

There are immeasurable ways in which Section 504's protections can come into play in a school setting, far beyond students who have 504 Plans. And your child does not need to have a 504 Plan to enjoy the antidiscrimination protections of 504. It applies to students with IEPs also—even to students who have disabilities but carry neither a 504 Plan nor an IEP.

Here are examples of a school district potentially violating Section 504 and discriminating against a child or his parents, even when it is not done in a mean-spirited way. All of the children in the following scenarios have disabilities.

1. Johnny loves to swim. He is really good at it, too! But Johnny can't use the school's pool. Why not? Because it's

booked throughout the day with regular education swim classes. Does that sound fair to you? It's not. It's also a likely 504 violation for discrimination.

2. Rosa is moving from fifth to sixth grade, which is a move from the elementary school to the middle school in her district. Her IEP team is planning her program for sixth grade. Her team has recommended that she receive an hour daily of special education direct instruction in order to receive a free and appropriate public education, to which she is legally entitled. Sex education is a course all students are expected to take in sixth grade. Unfortunately, it's scheduled during the period that the special education teacher is available to teach Rosa. The IEP team tells her parents that Rosa will have to skip sex education. Should a child have to choose between the special education services she requires and a subject so important it's mandated for all students who don't have disabilities in her grade? No. It's a probable 504 violation for discrimination.

3. Virginia is a sassy little eight-year-old. She loves to sing and act, and she has a beautiful singing voice. She wants to try out for the school production of Annie. The advisor to the acting club requires all students to read a five-page excerpt of the play for the audition. Virginia's IEP requires that all written material be provided to her in extremely large font because of her vision difficulties. Her parents ask that the excerpt be provided to her in this format so she can read the part. The advisor tells the parents that she does not have the ability to print out the excerpt in large font, and suggests that Virginia volunteer

to be part of the stage crew. In other words, because Virginia has a visual impairment, she isn't allowed to audition for the school play. This, too, is a 504 violation and discriminatory.

4. Justin attends Sunnyvale Elementary School, a lovely public school that encourages all parents to volunteer in the classrooms and help out in the cafeteria. The last time Justin's mom volunteered in the cafeteria, she noticed that, contrary to what she had been told in his IEP meetings, Justin was not interacting with any students and appeared to be totally socially isolated. She mentioned it to the team at her next meeting. A few days later she received a letter informing her that if she wanted to observe her son in school, she must schedule her visit in advance and sign in at the office. In addition, her observations would be limited to twice a year. Does an open door policy for parents of children who do not have disabilities but strict limitations on parents whose children have disabilities seem wrong? Yes, it does. This is a double whammy: it's a probable violation of 504 not just because of the discrimination, but since the letter came on the heels of Justin's mother's expressing concerns about his program, it's likely retaliation as well.

5. David uses a wheelchair. This requires special transportation, which he receives in order to go to and from school every day. In the entire time he has been in middle school, he has never been included in a single field trip. His mother is not made aware that field trips are scheduled until the day before the trip, when she receives

an email asking if she would like him to participate and if so, if she can drive him and serve as his 1:1 support. Just because an activity isn't happening in the school building does not insulate the school district from their obligation to include students with disabilities. This is a 504 violation, as David is being denied a benefit of the district because of his disability.

6. Ling is in eighth grade in a charter school. She spends most of her school day in a separate classroom where she receives her special education instruction and related services. She is included in the mainstream classroom for only fifteen minutes every day, during circle time in the morning. At the end of the school year, families are invited to a graduation ceremony for each classroom. Ling's parents and grandparents arrive, excited to watch Ling participate. Each child in the classroom is called up to the stage, one by one, and given a rose and a balloon. To the dismay of Ling's family, the class is formally announced after all of the students, except Ling, are on the stage. The teacher forgot Ling entirely, a painful oversight that is also a violation of federal law.

7. Dominic is unable to speak. He is assigned a 1:1 para-professional who accompanies him throughout his day at school. She sends home a note every day telling Dominic's parents how his day went. After several weeks of notes indicating that Dominic's behaviors were very severe and worrisome, his father emailed the Special Education Director, asking for an emergency IEP meeting, which was promptly scheduled. In the six school days between the email and the IEP meeting, no notes came home from

105

the para. At the IEP meeting, Dominic's parents asked about this and were informed that the notes would no longer come home because school district policy states that parents are not allowed to communicate directly with the paras since they are not certified staff. The one person who is able to tell the parents how their son's day is going, because he can't tell them himself, is now unable to speak with the parents. This is a trifecta: discrimination, retaliation, and intimidation. Oh my!

Each of these examples is real. And each of these parents can file OCR complaints, though that isn't always the best course of action (if you can't prove your allegations, for example). School districts are extremely intimidated by OCR filings, as they should be; the US Department of Education has great authority over schools, and can even freeze a district's federal funding. But there are many ways to ensure that these situations don't occur, or recur. Contact your special education administrator to inform her of the issue, and ask if a plan can be put in place to avoid these situations. It doesn't hurt if you mention that you're giving the district the opportunity to rectify the situation because you'd like to avoid the OCR filing.

What Your School District Isn't Telling You

They won't tell you about what we call "the big four": discrimination, retaliation, coercion, and intimidation. Technically, a policy, practice, or procedure of a school can be discriminatory toward people with disabilities without intending to be so, but retaliation, intimation, and coercion are claims that connote intentional conduct. If your school district is engaging in this type of conduct, it's not likely to go out of its way to tell you how to stop it or how to sue the district for it.

What Can You Do about It

Discrimination of any type is no laughing matter and not to be treated lightly. Don't allege it if it's not warranted. Throwing around terms like "discrimination" or "retaliation" will result in a permanent erosion of trust and credibility in your relationship with your child's school, so make sure you've done your homework *before* making any such allegations.

If you have reason to allege any of the big four, you could send this email if you want to avoid formal action, such as filing with the OCR:

Dear (insert administrator),

I am writing about a serious matter that I am hoping you can help be resolved. Let me explain the situation. (Explain factually here.)

I cannot help but feel that this is (insert retaliation/ discrimination/coercion/intimidation) against me given my efforts to advocate on behalf of my child, (insert name).

It is my understanding that I can file a complaint with the Office of Civil Rights regarding this matter.

107

At this juncture, I am trying to avoid taking that step and ask for you to resolve the matter. My proposed resolution is (insert requested remedy).

I look forward to hearing from you to learn how you would like to proceed.

Many thanks,

(insert your name)

cc: Director of Special Education

If the matter is not resolved and your district does not cooperate with you, you may want to consider submitting a complaint with the Office of Civil Rights (at http://www2.ed.gov/about/offices/list/ocr/docs/howto.pdf).

17

Procedural Safeguards

Jerry Seinfeld has a great quote: "We're all playing the game, but the lawyers have read the top of the box." The procedural safeguards are the rules that govern special education at the "top of the box."

If you've been to an IEP team meeting, you were probably handed your procedural safeguards at some point during that meeting, or should have at a minimum received them annually. Why? Because the school district has to provide them to you under the Individuals with Disabilities Education Act. They are legally obligated to do so.

While they are obligated to give them to you, they probably won't explain them to you. At best, an administrator will make a casual comment at the beginning of the IEP meeting stating that they have given you your rights and if you have questions, let them know. Why? The safeguards are highly complicated and, frankly, explain that you have a lot of rights. Your school district does not necessarily want you to understand them, let alone enforce them.

If you've actually read your procedural safeguards, consider yourself among the select few, as they are daunting. It is the kind of document that makes your eyes gloss over. Parents often tell us that they have received them but never read them. Even our lawyer clients tell us this.

So why are we devoting a chapter to the procedural safeguards? We want you to understand the rules you and the school must follow to ensure that your child receives a free appropriate public education (FAPE)—the cornerstone of special education.

The rules include making sure you get written notice of an action proposed or refused by the district before the school actually follows through on it; the fact that parents are required to be invited to their child's IEP meeting and that the district should do its best to get them there; how you can disagree with your school district over your child's program; timelines you and the school district must follow over disagreements and the procedures for resolving differences of opinion; when the school can remove your child from school, for how long, and for what reasons; the fact that you can ask that your child be maintained in the last program you agreed to when your school wants to change his program; and more. It is important information, and you should become as familiar with your procedural safeguards as you can.

School districts love to characterize the procedural safeguards as nitpicky and indeed, Congress has made it clear that small procedural violations will not lead to complete liability for school districts. In order for a procedural violation to matter, there has to be a demonstrated connection between that violation and a deprivation of FAPE. But as one court noted, Congress didn't require districts to follow the procedures as "mere hoops through which the school district should jump," but rather envisioned that full parental participation in the

110

development of a child's program and IEP would result in quality educational programming.

What Your School District Isn't Telling You

Yes, it will provide you with your procedural safeguards. If it hasn't already, it should! But it is not going to sit you down and explain them to you chapter and verse. The bottom line is that parents are often enforcing the IDEA. No one is waiting in line behind you to do the job. If you're going to enforce the IDEA, you're going to have to understand your procedural rights to do so.

What You Can Do about It

Remember this: your procedural safeguards guarantee that you, as parents, have an opportunity to 1) examine all records relating to your child; 2) to participate in meetings with respect to the identification, evaluation, and educational placement of your child and the provision of a free appropriate public education; and 3) to obtain an Independent Educational Evaluation of your child.

Happy reading.

18

You Shouldn't Have to Pay for That

Sally and Kate live across the street from each other and attend the same neighborhood public school. They both get on the same bus to school every school morning. In fact, they both have Mrs. Smith as their third grade teacher. Sally is a student who has a disability and Kate is not.

What if Sally's parents have to pay for transportation and her program at school, while Kate's parents do not? What is wrong with this picture?

Two children attending the same public school should not be treated differently from a financial perspective. In fact, in this hypothetical scenario, Sally is being discriminated against for having a disability and education services that might exceed the cost of Kate's.

This scenario demonstrates why you shouldn't have to pay for any part of your child's special education program, including evaluations to identify needs and services required for an appropriate education, related services deemed appropriate by the IEP team, specialized or regular transportation, and more.

Remember that the IDEA requires that students who have special education needs are entitled to a *Free* and Appropriate

Public Education, or a FAPE. If the educational services are not free, as they are to students who do not have special education needs, then it is simple discrimination.

What Your School District Isn't Telling You

When you offer to pay for or have already paid for a service, device, equipment, or an evaluation, your school district probably won't wrestle you to the ground and insist on reimbursing you for it. In fairness, can you blame them? You just saved them a lot of money. You'll be kept in the dark on the things your school may have to fund unless you become informed.

What You Can Do about It

Let's be clear: just because your child has a disability doesn't mean that the school district is responsible for paying for everything. School districts have a legal obligation to provide your child with a free appropriate public education, so anything that is linked to your child's school program and is agreed upon through the IEP should be provided at no cost to you. Don't think that the school has to pay for every imaginable service. Just as parents of children who do not have disabilities supplement their child's education with programs and equipment that are nice but not necessary, parents of children with special education needs can do the same. Programs and services must be a part of your child's special education plan in order to be funded by your district.

Ask yourself some questions when you want your district to cover or reimburse an expense as a part of your child's education. If it's an outside evaluation you're asking them to fund, ask yourself if the information and recommendations from the evaluation provide educational information that the school team does not have now that addresses a current or unmet need. If it's a service you want supported financially, ask yourself if this service will help your child learn a skill she doesn't have now but needs as a part of her education. If it's a device or equipment you want the district to pay for, ask yourself if it will help put your child on an even playing field with her nondisabled peers or help him perform an educational task or obtain a life skill he wouldn't otherwise obtain. These are not *legal* questions, the answers to which determine if the school should pay for the expense. Put yourself in the shoes of the school district to help you understand, and articulate, how the requested expenditure is educationally benefitting your child. The team will be asking themselves these questions; be prepared with the answers.

If you are convinced that the answers to these questions demonstrate that your child should have the service, evaluation, or equipment at public expense, stop paying for it yourself. At a minimum, submit a written request for reimbursement to your district. If these services may be a part of your school district's legal obligation to educate your child, formally request that the IEP team incorporate them into your child's IEP. If the district denies the request for reimbursement or funding, make sure your request is documented and that you preserved your right to disagree so you can consider formal action.

19

Can You Observe Your Child in School?

When you think about it, you should be able to observe your child in school. It's a public school supported by your tax dollars. Why wouldn't they let you in to observe? As it turns out, there may be plenty of reasons. The question becomes: are they legally allowed to bar you from observing?

One of the key purposes of the IDEA is to strengthen and expand the role of parents in the identification, evaluation, and educational placement of their child. The IDEA specifically provides that the parents of a child with disabilities:

1. Have an opportunity to participate in meetings with respect to the identification, evaluation, and educational placement of their child, and the provision of a free appropriate public education to their child.
2. Be part of any group that determines what additional data are needed as part of an evaluation of their child and determine their child's eligibility and educational placement.
3. Have their concerns and the information that they

provide regarding their child considered in developing and reviewing their child's IEP.

4. Be regularly informed, as specified in their child's IEP, at least as often as parents are informed of their nondisabled children's progress, of their child's progress toward the annual goals in the IEP and the extent to which that progress is sufficient to enable the child to achieve the goals by the end of the year.

In May 2004, Shari A. Mamas, a staff attorney at the Education Law Center in Pittsburg, Pennsylvania, sought guidance on observation in school from the Office of Special Education Programs (OSEP) in Washington, DC. These four tenets were cited in the OSEP's response.

The OSEP's letter states that the IDEA expects parents of children with disabilities to have a role in the evaluation and educational placement of their children and be participants, along with school personnel, in developing, reviewing, and revising the IEPs for their children. However, the statute and the regulations implementing the IDEA do not provide a general entitlement for parents of children with disabilities, or their professional representatives, to observe their children in any current classroom or proposed educational placement.

The letter explained that the determination of who has access to classrooms may be addressed by state and/or local policy. However, OSEP encourages school district personnel and parents to work together in ways that meet the needs of both the parents and the school, including providing opportunities for parents to observe their children's classrooms and proposed placement options. In addition, there may be circumstances in which access may need to be provided. For example, if parents invoke their right to an Independent Educational Evaluation of their child and the evaluation requires observing the child in the educational placement, the evaluator may need access to the placement.

To observe, show your school the OSEP letter, and we hope the observation gates open. We say "hope" because we realize that showing them the letter does not guarantee anything.

Here's the bottom line: you are legally entitled to observe your child in school for all of the reasons the OSEP letter cited. However, your right to do so is not unfettered, nor should it be. It doesn't make sense for parents to be able to wander into a school unannounced for any reason they choose, especially after the tragedy in Newtown, Connecticut. It is reasonable for schools to have observation policies that require parents to set up observations in advance and identify the reason why they would like to observe. Unfortunately, we see observation policies that fly in the face of the IDEA's four tenets that support observations all too often.

If your school district is giving you a hard time about observation, request a written copy of the district's observation policy. Parents often discover that the written policy differs from what they were told it was. There can be a big difference between the district's policy and what is practiced, so ask for the written policy. If the written policy doesn't jive with these tenants of the IDEA, you may want to pursue more formal action. Your written letter of request to observe should cite the four tenants of the IDEA that support your right to observe. Your letter of request should also capture how observing will help you understand your child's school program, which in turn helps you participate in the development of her IEP.

What Your School District Isn't Telling You

Many districts encourage parents to volunteer in class when their children are in their early school years. We think these volunteer hours provide great opportunities to help out in the classroom and provide the chance for you to observe how your child is functioning in school. These invitations usually come to a screeching halt by the third grade. Past that point school districts won't tell you they need your assistance in the class-room. Sadly, this is especially true for parents of children with disabilities, who are often put in a position of having to piece together information about their child's program, especially if their child cannot communicate with them at home about their school day. But continuing opportunities to see how your child is functioning in school is important.

What You Can Do about It

If it is important for you to observe your child, you will have to request to observe your child in writing. The email can go something like this:

Dear (insert principal),

As you may be aware, I am trying to learn as much as I can about (insert your child's name)'s school pro-gram through his/her IEP team meetings. It is very important for me to be able to understand his/her needs, strengths, and overall program so I can be a participant in the development of his/her IEP as we move forward.

It is helpful for me to review my child's progress toward his/her IEP goals and the curriculum when I receive his/her progress updates. Unfortunately, the data alone does not provide me with the level of understanding that an observation at school can provide me. I would like to see how he/she functions at school: academically, socially, emotionally, behaviorally, and adaptively.

I would like to see how (insert child's name) is doing in every aspect of his/her day. I realize it is not appropriate for me to come in and observe him/her for an entire day. I would like to come in and see each area of his/her day over time. I have attached my son's/ daughter's schedule with a proposed schedule of my observations. Please let me know if this works for you and his/her school team. If not, please propose some alternate options.

Many thanks,

(insert your name)

cc: Director of Special Education

If your school district denies you the ability to observe your child, here is a follow-up letter you can email to the principal and copy to the Director of Special Education:

> Dear (insert principal),
>
> It is disappointing that you have denied me the opportunity to observe my son/daughter, (insert name), in school. I have included an Office of Special Education (OSEP) guidance letter regarding parents observing their children in school. (Include the link as an option to embedding the entire letter in your email: www2.ed.gov/policy/speced/guid/idea/letters/2004-2/mamas052604placement2q2004.pdf)
>
> Would you also please provide me with the district's board of education–approved, written policy supporting your position that I will not be permitted to observe my child?
>
> In the meantime, I hope that you will reconsider your decision.
>
> Many thanks,
>
>
> (insert your name)
>
> cc: Director of Special Education

Make your observation count. Gather information that will help you and the school team improve upon your child's IEP. Know why you are observing. Do you suspect your child isn't playing purposefully on the playground or that he is sitting alone during lunch and unable to socialize appropriately? Are you concerned about her academic performance and how long it takes her to complete academic tasks as compared with her nondisabled peers? Do you think your child isn't being supported enough or supported too much? Are you observing to see concerning behaviors? You should have a sense of what you are going in to see before you observe so that you can document the answers to your questions.

You almost certainly won't be able to observe an entire day or see all things up close. You may have to observe from the sidelines or from a distance. Observing can be tricky, especially if your child performs differently when she knows you are there. Write down your questions and ask them after the observation, not during it. There may be a good pedagogical reason for something you observed. Finally, unless something is truly harming your child while you're observing, do *not* disrupt the educational environment or challenge the educators about their instruction while you are there. This will not only create tension, but will most certainly result in derailing the observation. Plus, you will play into the district's possible narrative that you are an unreasonable parent, which can only harm you in the end.

Once you have the information from your observation, meet with the team to discuss what you have seen. Remember that you will see things from your perspective, and the results of your observations must be held in balance with the team's perspectives. Share the good and the bad. Ask questions. Your observation helps you become a key member of your child's team and should help you understand what you need to know.

20

Scheduling IEP Meetings

Of course meetings should be scheduled when you can attend! How often does your school district ask when it would be convenient for you to have the IEP team meeting? We're guessing you would say "never." We haven't experienced most districts putting a premium on courtesy to parents on this issue.

In fact, the IDEA's provisions on scheduling IEP team meetings involve common sense and courtesy. They are written to ensure that parents have an opportunity to attend the meeting and contribute. The bottom line is that the school and parents have to agree on when and where they are going to meet.

Here's what the IDEA says: "Each public agency must take steps to ensure that one or both of the parents of a child with a disability are present at each IEP Team meeting or are afforded the opportunity to participate. . . . This includes: (1) Notifying parents of the meeting early enough to ensure that they will have an opportunity to attend; and (2) Scheduling the meeting at a mutually agreed on time and place."

Early on in her child's IEP career, Julie received notices stating when an IEP team meeting was scheduled. Since they were never scheduled when she could attend, she set out on a mission to make sure the school district sought her availability first. Julie sent an email to the Director of Special Education politely requesting that she be afforded the courtesy of receiving a phone call or email seeking her availability on a particular date and time. She added, "I am aware that the IDEA requires that parent and the school must schedule meetings at a mutually agreed upon time."

At first, Julie's approach didn't work. However, after rejecting the date every time the school assigned a meeting without checking with her, the school began to get the message. After having to reschedule four IEP team meetings, the school began to contact her before assigning a date and time.

Julie never stopped appreciating the phone call she would get asking for her available dates for the IEP meetings. It made her feel like a valued member of the process. We wish more school districts would take note of this. The simplest of things can make such a big difference!

What Your School District Isn't Telling You

Your school district might not let you know that scheduling the IEP meeting is not a unilateral matter; it must be done in cooperation with you. Instead, you will probably get the invitation without consideration of your availability. It will probably be an announcement of when the meeting will occur, rather than an offer with options of when it could occur. If you happen to be available for the time and date they have selected, by all means, confirm the meeting. But if you're not, you do not need to accept the scheduled date for the meeting.

What You Can Do about It

There is a saying that you can't change someone else's behavior until you've changed your own. This sample email informs the school that you will no longer accept an approach that ignores your availability. It tells your district that you would like to be treated with courtesy. We suggest you copy the Director of Special Education because you cannot assume that the person doing the scheduling has a full understanding of their obligations under the IDEA. The Director of Special Education should be the person in the district who has such understanding.

> Dear (insert principal or person who schedules your IEP team meetings),
>
> Unfortunately, I typically receive notices of my son's/daughter's IEP team meetings with no consideration of my/our availability. I hope you can appreciate how frustrating this is when it is very important to me/us to be able attend my son's/daughter's IEP meetings and have notice so I /we can arrange my/our schedule(s).
>
> I have recently learned that the IDEA requires the school district to consider our availability:
>
> "Each public agency must take steps to ensure that one or both of the parents of a child with a disability are present at each IEP Team meeting or are afforded the opportunity to participate. . . . This includes: (1) Notifying parents of the meeting early enough to

ensure that they will have an opportunity to attend; and (2) Scheduling the meeting at a mutually agreed on time and place."

In the future, please do not secure my son's/daughter's IEP team meetings without considering my/our availability. Unfortunately, I will be forced to reschedule any meetings that have been scheduled without consideration of my/our availability. I certainly don't want to put your team in the position of having to repeatedly reschedule, so I am sure you'll agree that it is easier to coordinate our schedules at the outset.

I can be reached at (insert email) and (insert phone number).

Many thanks,

(insert your name)

cc: Director of Special Education

Remember that you are simply exercising your rights, and that your child will benefit from your doing so.

21

Special Education
Urban Legends Exposed

Simply saying something over and over again should not make people think it's true, but it does. There are so many myths in special education that a whole book could be devoted to them. These urban legends often are not being repeated to mislead a parent; the educators themselves actually believe them to be true. But they aren't, and they can truly result in harm for many kids. We have demystified these legends for you, and are telling the truth instead.

Myth: **Only intellectually disabled kids get special ed.**
           If we've heard it once, we've heard it a thousand times. Parents are told, "Your child is too smart for special education." Or the other oldie but goodie, "Your child would never qualify for special education because he gets good grades." No matter how you say it, or how many times you say it, it's wrong as a matter of fact and law.

Truth: **Smart kids can receive special education.**

Myth: **Your school can force you to medicate your child.**
The IDEA includes a very clear statement on the pro-hibition on mandatory medication: ". . . The State educational agency shall prohibit State and local educational agency personnel from requiring a child to obtain a prescription for a substance covered by the Controlled Substances Act . . . as a condition of attending school, receiving an evaluation . . . or receiving services under this title." Despite this fed-eral guidance, teachers and school staff will suggest to parents that they give their child medication. They can't, by law.

Truth: **Your school can't tell you that your child has to be on medication.**

Myth: **We have to have the IEP meeting before the school year ends.**
Many children with disabilities qualify for spe-cial education services during the summer because either they will regress without the services or the nature and severity of their disability requires sum-mer instruction. Schools routinely tell parents their children don't qualify for summer services and if by some miracle they do qualify, put programs together that don't provide a free appropriate pub-lic education.

Truth: **Services are available and meetings happen over the summer.**

Myth: **Parents like to be called "Mom" or "Dad" by the team.**

130

Don't. Call. Me. Mom. Among the many things that schools unwittingly do to diminish parents is to refer to them as "Mom" and "Dad." Most IEP teams are comprised of ten to twenty members of staff around the table. Everyone is referred to by their names, except for the parents who are most often referred to by their role. Parents have names and want to be called by them.

Truth: **Parents want to be called by their names.**

Myth: **Parents have to document regression to get summer services.**

School districts must provide extended school year (ESY) services under certain circumstances. Parents typically think of these as summer services. The IDEA notes that if a child requires ESY to receive a free appropriate public education, she must get it and it must be individualized. However, parents are often told that the only way kids get ESY services is if regression has previously been documented, and worse, they must prove the regression. This is just not so. For many students, the nature and severity of their disability requires programming year round. Many states have provided guidance to this effect, but be prepared to counter this urban legend. And if you happen to have proof of regression, feel free to share it.

Truth: **ESY services are provided to students who require it for FAPE.**

Myth: **If your child misbehaves in school you have to pick him up.**

131

We can't tell you how often clients of ours with IEPs miss school because their parents are told to pick him up early, drop him off late, or otherwise limit the school day because his behavior interferes with his ability to follow school rules. There are so many ways in which this is inappropriate, educationally and legally, that it's hard to know where to start. At a minimum, the parent should ask the school to do a Functional Behavior Assessment (even though the school should have thought of it) and schedule an IEP meeting to ascertain what is causing the behavioral challenges. But "call mom to get him" is not a plan.

Truth: **Calling parents to pick up their child is not a behavior plan.**

Myth: **All medical testing is the parents' responsibility.**
While it is true that medical *treatment* is not a school district's obligation, if a medical diagnosis is necessary in order to determine a child's needs, that diagnosis qualifies as a "related service" under the IDEA. So if you suspect ADHD but nobody on the team is qualified to issue that diagnosis, you can ask the IEP team to refer your child for that evaluation. Same for auditory and visual concerns. We've even had districts refer a child for testing to rule out seizures. This information is necessary for the district to have, and while we encourage parents to offer their insurance coverage as a courtesy, it is ultimately an

obligation of the school team to obtain an outside medical diagnosis if it's necessary to provide the child with a free appropriate public education.

Truth: **You can ask for a medical evaluation.**

Myth: **The only reason we reevaluate is to determine eligibility.**

At least every three years a school district must reevaluate your child in all suspected areas of disability, and determine if she remains eligible for special education services, and if so, under what category. Somehow, over time, this mandate morphed into an urban legend that school districts conduct this testing *only* to determine if a child still qualifies for services, which has resulted in thousands of children not being retested. The school says to the parents at triennial time, "We all know he's eligible, so why put him through the testing?" Most parents unknowingly agree. Why is this a problem? Because the testing also documents progress, or lack thereof; the testing should be conducted in all suspected areas of disability, which often over time reveal new areas of need that would be missed if the test were skipped; and as students age, they may need to use that testing to enter adult services or supports. Do not give in to the suggestion to skip triennial testing because you believe that its only purpose is to see if your child will still have an IEP.

Truth: **Triennials aren't just to determine eligibility.**

What Your School District Isn't Telling You

Because educators believe many of these urban legends, they might not tell you any of these things aren't true because they don't know it themselves.

What You Can Do about It

Don't believe something just because it's said repeatedly. Google it, call your state's Parent Information and Training Center (find it at www.parentcenterhub.org/find-your-center/), call your state's department of special education and, when all else fails, ask your school district for the written authority supporting its directive.

If what the district has advised is in alignment with the IDEA, move ahead with its directive. If not, let it know that you have conflicting information and that you intend to follow the written, federal authority on the matter.

22

Getting Ready for Primetime: Transition to Adulthood

We don't need a study to demonstrate that strong parent advocacy changes outcomes for children. We know it isn't fair. It stinks that you have to go above and beyond what parents of a child in regular education have to do to make sure your child is getting an appropriate education. But remember that how prepared your child is for adulthood is at the heart of the IDEA's purpose: "To ensure that all children with disabilities have available to them a free appropriate public education that emphasizes special education and related services designed to meet their unique needs and prepare them for further education, employment, and independent living." We simply can't remind you of this enough: "further education, employment, and independent living."

It's never too early to start thinking about your child's adulthood. Many parents of children with disabilities are so overwhelmed with the daily obligations of parenting, in combination with the advocacy they've taken on with their school district and perhaps their insurance company, they forget to look very far down the road. Your child's adulthood will happen before you know it! One day your child will graduate, be "exited" (no longer meet criteria for eligibility), or age out of the protective environment of school and the rights afforded her under the IDEA. The teaching and interventions will come to an end, and hopefully your child will have the skills needed to be an independent adult. Transition is supposed to be a results-oriented process that provides your young adult child with skills, skills, and more skills—skills for further education, employment, and/or independent living.

In accordance with the IDEA, the term *transition services* means a coordinated set of activities for a child with a disability that:

- Is focused on improving the academic and functional achievement of the child with a disability to facilitate the child's movement from school to post-school activities, including postsecondary education, vocational education, integrated employment (including supported employment), continuing and adult education, adult services, independent living, or community participation
- Is based on the individual child's needs, taking into account the child's strengths, preferences, and interests
- Includes instruction, related services, community experiences, the development of employment and other post-school adult living objectives, and, if appropriate, acquisition of daily living skills and functional vocational evaluation

That's overwhelming. Think of it this way: you can't know how to get somewhere unless you know where you are going. So let's start at the beginning.

When to start, when to start? As a matter of federal law, transition services must be included in all IEPs when a student reaches age sixteen, and may be included for younger students if deemed appropriate by the IEP team. Some states begin the transition process sooner, and require that it be addressed by the IEP in place by the student's fourteenth birthday. Check with your state's Department of Education to learn about your state's laws and if your child's transition program is required to begin earlier than at age sixteen. We believe the earlier the better when it comes to transition services. Unfortunately, we have seen many parents who don't understand what transition services are or that their child may be eligible for them.

What Your School District Isn't Telling You

Your school district may give you many pieces of misinformation because the area of transition is rife with misunderstanding. Here are the inaccurate perceptions of transition obligations that top our list:

1. "We don't need to do transition-specific assessments beyond what we do for all of our high school students." What does this mean? Your school district's high school might conduct interest inventories for all of its students in preparation for post–high school life. For example, Naviance (https://naviance.com) is a commonly used career readiness program used by schools to align student strengths and interests to postsecondary goals, improving student outcomes and connecting learning to life. While we encourage students to participate in assessments like this designed for all students, they do

not replace the need for further disability or transition-specific assessments in alignment with your child's needs.

2. "Your child isn't disabled enough to qualify for transition services. Transition is only for very disabled kids." No, no, no, and no! Nowhere in the IDEA does it say this. In fact, the law is quite clear that all students with IEPs are required to receive transition services. If your child has a learning disability and is headed off to college, her team should consider what kind of transition programming she may require. Does she know how to access the disability office at her college? Does she know how to take notes adequately, prioritize long-term assignments, and manage studying? Her team may decide that she needs specific assessments and goals to ensure the skills she will need to be successful in college. A student who profiles like this may not need independent living goals, but that doesn't mean she doesn't qualify at all. What specific transition services your child requires is up the IEP team, with your involvement.

What You Can Do about It

If your school district shuts you down over your request for transition assessments beyond regular education transition assessments or consideration of transition at all, you have no choice but to proceed with a letter to your Director of Special Education.

Dear (insert Director of Special Education),

I need to make you aware of a matter regarding my child, (insert name), who attends (insert school) and is in the (insert grade). I'm hoping that by bringing this matter to your attention you can help me resolve it. I would like to avoid filing a complaint with the state Department of Education, so I truly appreciate your help.

It is my understanding that my daughter is entitled to a free appropriate public education (FAPE) under the IDEA, which includes, at her age, her right to transition services:

"The purposes of IDEA include ensuring that all children with disabilities have available to them a free appropriate public education (FAPE) that emphasizes special education and related services designed to meet their unique needs and prepare them for further education, employment and independent living."

Would you please provide me with the district's written policy, approved by the board of education, supporting the team's decision not to offer my child, who has an IEP, transition services. Also, would you please provide me with any other written authority that supports the district's position to deny me my requests regarding transition?

I appreciate your help and guidance as I move forward in my efforts to resolve this matter. I look forward to hearing from you.

Many thanks,

(insert your name)

Be sure to follow up with the Director of Special Education to confirm that your child will receive the transition services she needs.

Part 3: Where the Rubber Meets the Road

Now you know what your school district won't tell you about what happens in special education decision making. You hopefully have a solid understanding of what motivates the action that your school district is, or is not, taking with your child. Now what? We want you to use that knowledge and *apply* it to advocating for your child. This is, indeed, the hardest part.

It's one thing to know your rights and have an inside view of what goes on in public schools. It's entirely another to sit in an IEP meeting or at your computer ready to email your administration and to know what to do.

In this last section, we will give you the tools you need to produce positive, *effective* outcomes for your child's education.

23

Demystify the Paperwork

One of the biggest obstacles to parents being able to effectively advocate for their child is a basic ignorance of what the paperwork means. Between the acronyms, small font, nonsensical definitions, and edu-speak, it's a wonder any parent ever leaves an IEP meeting with any idea of what they have agreed to or not. Add to that the fact that, even though federal law mandates and guides the ways in which the IEP must be written, each state has its own particular forms, and some simply leave it up to your local school district to decide how to design the IEP paperwork.

One of the most important things for you to do is to familiarize yourself with the IEP forms used by your child's school district. Hopefully, those forms are available on your state Department of Education's website. Many times they can be found under the category or link for educators, rather than parents. Feel free to go into that section; indeed, some of the most useful and telling information you can get is in the part of the website designed for educators. You may want to print out documents that you find useful (in addition to the forms), such as guidance from your state to school districts that may run afoul of the practices mandated by state and federal special education laws. Having a printed-out document that says "x" is the law when your local school district is telling you that "y" is the law can come in handy at an IEP meeting.

Read the forms on the website thoroughly, even if they are blank. See if your state has a handbook for parents or educators that explains what the forms are for and how to fill them out. Along with finding them online, you may find them sent home with the invitation to the IEP meeting.

If you live in a school district that uses its own forms instead the state's forms (usually a sign that there will be bigger problems later, in our experience), spend a good amount of time reading your child's previous IEPs. (This is good advice even if the school district uses the state's forms.) They will show you where the district documented requests in the past, and will guide you on how to ask to have your requests reflected in the IEP going forward. For example, if your child was assigned a 1:1 support person in the past, and you know this service was listed on a certain page of the IEP and how it was listed, and you want that support to continue, ask that it be similarly reflected in the IEP.

We know that reading through the fine print of these documents is almost as exciting as reading car rental agreements. But you will be at even more of a disadvantage than you already are as a parent if you remain in the dark about what the IEP needs to include, and what all that mumbo jumbo really means. The devil really is in the details.

What Your School District Isn't Telling You

Your school district will probably not tell you, unless you ask, how to use the district's IEP forms.

What You Can Do about It

Read the IEP forms online. Read what the IDEA says must be included on the IEP forms. Go to the IDEA website to find this information. There is no getting away from these basics. Go to these sites, read these model forms, and compare them to your forms. Every state's forms are different and change frequently. Though tedious, this exercise will open your eyes and help you understand what information your school district must include on your child's IEP.

24

We Have a Form for That!

If your school team tells you that "we have a form for that," it's time for your antenna to go up. We understand that forms can be great tools. They allow all of us to streamline processes and help us avoid reinventing the wheel every time a common action needs to be taken, like permission for evaluations or a meeting or a service to proceed. Forms also allow larger districts to ensure some consistency across schools. From a parent perspective, it can be reassuring to have familiar forms to rely upon, rather than having to decipher new documents that differ annually. However, there is a real risk that a form will contain inaccurate, misleading, or incomplete information, sometimes even blatant misstatements of the law, which then becomes perpetuated across schools, parents, districts, and years.

Many forms are developed by committees of educators, who often do not have the benefit of legal advice while developing them.

For example, let's say your team is discussing Extended School Year (ESY) services to determine if your child should continue the IEP over the summer. The person chairing the meeting says, "Let's go through the ESY eligibility check list." Unfortunately, these forms have wrongly justified not providing ESY services to many unsuspecting parents, misstating the true standard for when a child is eligible for ESY services and flying in the face of the IDEA.

The result? By using an improper form, your child, who might otherwise qualify for summer services, doesn't get them.

Here's another example. You disagreed with the school district's evaluation of your child and have requested an IEE (Independent Educational Evaluation). The chairperson then says, "Let's see what our team thinks." After the discussion the chairperson announces that the team will fill out a form that determines if their district evaluations met the criteria for a thorough evaluation.

The form has questions like this:

- Did the evaluation follow all of the individual assessment protocols? Yes or No
- Did the evaluation include a list of all of the assessments? Yes or No
- Did the evaluation include a parent interview? Yes or No
- Did the evaluator possess the appropriate education, training, and experience required to conduct the specific evaluation? Yes or No

The problem is that the answers to these questions may not, in fact, have any legal or even factual relevance to the question of whether the parent is entitled to the IEE! As a result, your child may not receive the IEE you believe is necessary.

Other forms can be overinclusive, listing items to be checked off that have no bearing on the question at hand. For example, a form says that the parent is waiving the participation of a certain IEP team member, but for reasons that are unclear, includes a statement that the parents agree with that person's draft goals (goals proposed by the educators but not yet agreed upon by the IEP team). Or a form that gives consent to provide special education instruction in general, but states that the parent is in agreement with the proposed IEP, which is an entirely different question.

Not only do we believe that forms like these can be misleading, we also believe that they can serve to intimidate parents. Why? Because the nature of forms, combined with the power dynamic between parents who are sitting by themselves and a table full of educators, encourages parents to sign forms without necessarily reading them. The casual nature of, "Oh, that's just our form" may lead to a parent unknowingly forfeiting significant rights on behalf of their child.

Finally, just because it's an official-looking form doesn't mean that it has been well crafted, that it is in compliance with the IDEA, or that it is reliable. Indeed, many of the forms we've disputed over the years were created by state Departments of Education and distributed to local school districts for their use. The local districts rightly assume that state forms will pass legal muster, but they very well may not. Indeed, the federal government has many times directed individual states to revise or eliminate forms they have created that are legally erroneous. Just having the header of an educational agency and state seal on the document does *not* equal legitimacy.

What Your School District Isn't Telling You

Your school district won't say, "This form completely violates your rights, but we've used it for years and it works like a charm pulling the wool over parents' eyes every time." Nor will they say, "Nobody who has any credentials to determine the legality of this form has ever looked at it." They likely don't know that themselves!

What You Can Do about It

Read this to yourself five times and then read it aloud another five times: "I will not sign any form without taking the time to read it, understand it, and if necessary, get legal advice on it." It goes against the comfort level of virtually every person who has ever been asked to sign a form but it is critical to your child's education.

Do not give in to the pressure of the team telling you to sign a form without reading it. Ask if you can take it home with you and get back to them in a few days after reviewing it. Know that the team will likely try to reject your request. They may even try to use the threat that your child won't get what he needs unless you sign it. Your internal mantra will be: "I will not sign any form without taking the time to read it, understand it, and if necessary, get legal advice on it." And you will politely decline to sign if you can't honestly say you've read it, understood it, and obtained professional advice if you don't, or if your gut tells you something is off.

You may feel compelled to sign a form and you do so without reviewing it. If this happens (and we've all done it), sign the form but state for the record something like this: "I would like my concern regarding signing the form to be reflected on the record under parent concerns. While I signed the form, let the record reflect that I did not have the opportunity to review the form in its entirety and that I maintain the right to change my mind upon reading it further."

For better or worse, forms play an important role in your child's education. Make sure you understand them before you sign them.

25

Bring Your A Game

The sad reality is that parents are not on an even playing field with their child's school district. The school has built-in experts; creates, holds, and maintains the educational records; has full-day access to observing the child in school; has training on educational methodology; and knows the system far better than the average parent. If you don't want to be at a huge disadvantage in the process of securing appropriate services for your child, you're going to have to be *more* equipped to discuss your child's program, *more* current on your child's needs, and *more* organized in presenting your arguments than the school team. There are no guarantees, but it's a lot more likely that your child will get what she needs if you are.

So how do you bring your A game. As with many things in life, preparation goes a long, long way. Here are the four most important things you can do to prepare to persuade your school team that your child requires the services you believe will be effective:

1. Focus on facts, not feelings. It's okay to have strong intuition about what your child needs; most parents do, regardless of whether or not their child has a disability.

But in the context of an IEP team meeting, "I just think he needs it" won't cut it. You need demonstrable evidence and must be able to articulate why your child should get the program you believe is appropriate. In addition to having outside, independent evaluators who can help substantiate the need (which is the most effective way to prove your point, in our opinion), organize your child's records. Graph and chart the data in your child's educational records. Start by looking at IEP goals: do many of them repeat year after year without mastery, or with only slight wording changes? Putting that data into a graph or chart can be very powerful. Simply doing the math on IEP paperwork can be effective as well. For example, if the district proposes as a plan to address behavior that your child leave school twenty minutes early every day, add it up. Twenty minutes a day times 180 school days is 3,600 minutes of missed instruction. That's sixty hours of missed instruction! Now tabulate what percentage of the school day and school year that means your child is missing. If you can come prepared with information like this in a data-driven, nonemotional way, you are far more likely to make your point, and make it well.

2. Be emotionally prepared. Nothing is more important to a parent than her child. It is impossible, therefore, to be objective about your child. This means most parents walk into IEP meetings, which are already inherently stressful and overwhelming for many, feeling emotional; and we all know that it's hard to make good, rational decisions when you feel that way. Worse, many parents are completely intimidated by the process. There's something

about how most of us were raised to respect authority (and let's face it, school teachers and administrators were the first profession that most of us were taught to obey) that can turn intelligent and competent parents into cowering schoolchildren once again. This is especially so when your district has a dozen or so educators sitting around a table and the parent is alone. Being prepared will go a long way toward lessening the intimidation. In addition, try to have a calming technique in your mind that will allow you to not get off track. Imagine bluebirds singing in the background a la Snow White, even if you are really feeling more like Braveheart! If it's possible, have both parents present for emotional support (and keep in mind that fathers are often treated with more deference by the school team than mothers, in our experience). And of course, if you realize you are going to be emotional, call in a professional advocate or trusted friend to accompany you to the meeting.

3. Know what they will say. Jen tells her clients that she listens to everything the team tells her with one half of her body hearing it as a parents' attorney and the other half as a board attorney. This is how she protects their case. You can't know how to win an argument if you don't anticipate what the other arguments might be against yours. For this reason, you need to walk into any IEP meeting where you will be requesting services, evaluations, or programs on your child's behalf ready to respond to the school's reasons to say no. Ask yourself well in advance of the meeting, "What will they say when I ask for this?" Compile a list of what you will request

from the team. Then think about the key educators and administrators at the meeting and try to anticipate what they will say. Will someone argue they have tried a particular program before and it didn't work for your child? If the answer is "Yes, but that's because that educator was out sick half the year and it was never done consistently," be prepared to point out that the previous time it was offered it wasn't done with fidelity and you can't make conclusions as a result. Or was the goal written poorly with no demonstrable skill to observe or measure? Is the usual answer to your request, "We don't see that here"? If so, be armed with numerous examples of similar concerns that *are* documented (for example, you were called six times by the school to pick your child up because of behavior; there were ten incident reports in the last two months; when you dropped off her violin she was doing the same thing you are talking about; other parents or children are reporting things to you; and so on.) You can also point out that, "If he can do it at school but can't show that skill at home or in the community, we don't consider the skill mastered." It's usually fairly easy to anticipate what their rationale will be for saying no; be ready with your follow-up. And if you find yourself in a situation where no rationale is offered for their refusal or denial of your request, ask for the rationale for the decision. You'd be surprised how often there isn't one that can be articulated well.

4. Know what you will say: To the extent you can, have a planned response for obstacles that may be thrown in your way. For example, teams often say, "our policy is" as

justification for their actions. If we have heard it once we have heard it ten thousand times: when a parent requests a certain program, service, evaluation, or accommodation, the district will say no and invoke their "policy" as the reason. If an educator ever tells you the reason she can't or won't do something, or must do something, because of "policy," your immediate response should be, "May I have a copy of that policy please?" More often than not, the policy is not a policy (which requires a vote , typically by a governing body, and is in writing) and in fact is a *practice* of the team, school, or district. If indeed there is a written policy dictating what they can or can't do with kids with disabilities, it is often in violation of state or federal law. Most school districts have all of their school board policies online. Print them out and read them. They come in handy more often than you might think.

What Your School District Isn't Telling You

You are entitled to hire a special education advocate or attorney to attend IEP team meetings with you, to advise you or represent you or your child. If you cannot afford to hire a private professional in this capacity, look for agencies and nonprofit organizations that offer these services at little or no cost.

What You Can Do about It

Beyond focusing on the facts and not feelings, being emotionally prepared, and knowing what they and you will say, what can you do to bring your A game? A good place to start is to get into the habit of always recording your IEP team meeting. *Before* you do, however, check to see if recording the IEP team meeting is legal and permissible in your state, and if it is, *never* record the meeting without letting the team know you are doing so. Your state Department of Education or your Parent Information and Training Center should be able to tell you your state's rules about recording IEP meetings.

If you don't record, make sure you have someone with you who can be your extra set of eyes and ears and is good at taking notes. This is important because it's nearly impossible to remember everything that was said during the meeting. Recording the meeting—whether electronically or in writing—allows you to have evidence of what was actually said or decided upon in case you have a difference of opinion or recollection after the meeting as to what happened.

This letter will help you address recording the IEP meeting:

> Dear (insert name of person who chairs your meetings),
>
> We are looking forward to attending the IEP team meeting for (insert child's name) on (insert date).
>
> I wanted to let you know that I will be audio taping (insert child's name) meeting. (You may want to include an explanation, but you don't need to do so. The explanation could be 1) As you can imagine, IEP team meetings can be very overwhelming

and it is impossible for me to remember everything that happened at the meeting and the decisions that were made. Audio taping allows me to review the meeting, which is helpful to me; or 2) My husband/wife/partner/someone else is unable to attend the meeting with me and I want him/her to have the benefit of knowing what was discussed at the meeting.)

I wanted to let you know in advance so you would be prepared in the event that you would like to audio tape the meeting as well.

Many thanks,

(insert your name)

If you know in your heart of hearts that you simply don't have the courage and strength to do the hard work and take on your district when you advocate for your child, it may be time for you to retain a special education advocate or special education attorney to assist you. Your state's Parent Information and Training Center should have a list of advocates and attorneys. Another excellent source is the Council of Parent Attorneys and Advocates website (COPAA.org). COPAA is a national organization that protects the legal and civil rights of students with disabilities, and you can search the site by state. You may want to check out COPAA's Guidelines to Choosing a Special Education Advocate.

We also highly recommend asking other parents who they have used. Disability-specific organizations often maintain lists and have listservs that parents can join. Listservs let you ask parents throughout your state for input about advocates and attorneys.

26

Know the Players

There is something to be said for the expression, "It's not what you know, it's who you know" (although we think it's also darned important what you know). In the field of special education, *who* is involved in a child's case can make a tremendous difference. Administrative decisions can appear arbitrary; one evaluator might be willing to recommend intensive services while another in the same building won't; disciplinary matters are treated one way in a certain school and entirely another way in a school in the same town. All of this can become the culture of a school or district, and it's necessary for you to know what yours is if you want to operate effectively within it, or better yet, to change it if necessary.

When parents call us from districts or schools that are well-known to us in a negative fashion (districts that are repeat offenders of the IDEA or Section 504), we often have to tell them that they aren't just fighting a legal battle, they are dealing with a negative school culture. In some places, the culture has existed for years and is hard to turn around. We can get services, evaluations, and programs in place for a child, but it's near impossible to change the hearts and minds of the people in a school that doesn't want to do right by kids with disabilities.

So how do you determine a school's culture and then deal with it? If you are new to your town or school, ask around. Which administrators are fair and which aren't? Are there particularly skilled staff in certain schools versus another? Speak to parents of children with disabilities. How does the principal at a particular school treat not just children with disabilities, but their parents? Many school systems are tremendously successful for nondisabled students but not so for kids with special education needs. This information can help you avoid pitfalls of unhealthy or unproductive relationships within the team. Just as the parent of any child wants to know what the word on the street is about their child's classroom teacher, you should try to get information from other parents about the educators in your child's life.

We know what you're thinking: even if you find out which people are good and which are not so good, you don't get to pick and choose the ones you like. You're right. But this knowledge can make a big difference to your child. Consider course selection in middle and high school. Before you attend the IEP meeting where it will be discussed whether your child will take a foreign language, wouldn't you want to know if the Spanish teacher is dually certified in special education? If you are trying to decide whether to have your elementary-aged child receive speech services in the morning or later in the day, wouldn't you want to know that the morning speech teacher has a bad reputation when you answer that question? Dozens of decisions can be impacted by knowing the quality, attitude, and experiences of the educators in your child's school. Ask around.

You need to learn the background of possible outside evaluators as well. At some point in your child's education you or your school district may undertake an IEE (Independent Educational Evaluation). As noted earlier, there are many outside evaluators who are heavily connected to your school district or its lawyer. They may get paid the majority of their income by school districts and do not want to alienate them by making recommendations contrary to the school's interests. You need to find out who those evaluators are so you can avoid them.

Likewise, there are some evaluators perceived as being completely willing to say whatever a parent wants. That may or may not be a good thing for your case. On the one hand, you'll get a written recommendation you may like; on the other, the school is unlikely to be persuaded by it. And if it's someone really known to be a hired gun for parents, he may not help you as an evaluator because he is perceived as biased. We're not saying you should never use such an evaluator, but you need to know what could happen if you do.

If you find yourself formally engaging in the legal processes outlined for disputes under the IDEA of either mediation or a due process hearing, you also need to become informed about the people involved in those forums. It's important to know who the mediators or hearing officers are. Are they experienced? Patient? Understanding? Do you trust that they aren't aligned with the district and that they will fully hear your concerns? Likewise, what is the reputation of the lawyer who represents your school district? Is she easy to work with, or the opposite? We speak with parents every day who naively began the legal process with their district and walked into a highly complex piece of litigation against aggressive and skilled lawyers, when all they wanted was a simple evaluation. Knowledge is power, and you want as much of it as you can get.

Some savvy parents reach far out to know the players. Every year, we each field numerous calls and emails through our websites from parents who want to check with us before moving to a town in Connecticut because they had special education disputes where they live, and wish they had known which places to avoid before they moved the last time. We can't give them a definitive answer because at any given time a Director of Special Education could move, or other changes could be made in a district that completely change the landscape of that system. But it's still valuable to get the insights of local professionals who understand special education advocacy in your state. If you rely on your realtor to know, you're bound to be disappointed. Talk to other parents; join listservs; network. Indeed, if it weren't for parents joining forces, we wouldn't have federal laws to protect children with disabilities in the first place!

What Your School District Isn't Telling You

School districts aren't going to provide you with resumes and curricula vitae for their staff, and they're not going to tell you if a particular person has damaging information in his personnel file. Conversely, they will not tell you of the wonderful praises in his personnel file. They are not legally permitted to discuss personnel matters with you even if they were so inclined.

What You Can Do about It

Ask other parents about their experiences with staff members. Know, however, that just because another parent had a good,

164

or even bad, experience with a staff member does not mean your experience will be the same. If you have good instincts about someone, and over time, her performance and attitude prove positive with your child, you don't need to inquire further. But if your gut is telling you something is wrong, you should share your concerns with the principal, the Director of Special Education, or other administrator in writing. If a personality conflict is truly getting in the way of a productive relationship for your child or impeding his ability to receive an appropriate education, you need to address the situation immediately.

27

Toothless IEP Language

In virtually every lawsuit involving a child with an IEP where the court must determine if the parents' or the school district's view of the child's education is accurate, the court will start with the IEP. The IEP functions much like a contract between the parent and the school district, and just like with a contract, language matters. We hope you never find yourself in a courtroom looking at the language of your child's IEP in litigation. But you still need to be able to hold your school district accountable for following your child's IEP. And if the IEP itself is nebulous, or has language that is so up for interpretation as to be meaningless, you are never going to be able to do that. Worse, the educators working with your child won't know what they are supposed to do in order for your child to receive free and appropriate public education.

We get a pang in our gut every time we hear or read certain phrases in IEPs because we know all too well they mean almost nothing and allow for too much wiggle room. This slippery language gives no assurance that a program will be carried out with fidelity, or even at all. For example:

1. "As needed," as in "Johnny will receive behavioral support as needed." This means he may never need it and may never get it.

2. "Up to," as in "Up to ten hours of instruction per week." So anything under ten is okay. Like none?
3. "Access to," as in "Sally will have access to assistive technology in the classroom." Well, so do all the other kids. How is that individualized and how often will she use it, if ever?
4. "Upon request," as in "Mika will receive extra time upon request." Whose request? What if she doesn't ask for it but needs it?
5. "With assistance," as in "With assistance, Ryan will button his top button." How much assistance? What, if *anything*, will Ryan have gained as a skill by the end of a year with this kind of support?
6. "With hand-over-hand assistance," as in "With hand-over-hand assistance, Joanna will brush her hair." Think about this one; is Joanna doing anything here? An expert I like calls this the "dead man's test." If it can be accomplished on a dead person, then it has no role in an IEP!

These are not the only examples of language that can be written into IEPs which, when considered, render the service, accommodation, or recommendation useless. You want to avoid language like this. Ask your team to make the language clearer and specify the frequency and duration of the service as required by law; you should also remind the team of the importance of the IEP. If an educator responds with, "That's how it's written, but he always gets the ten hours," point out that the document should make clear to whoever picks it up what the program is—not what it could be, might be, or can be, subject to the mood or interpretation of whoever is reading it. Keep in mind that you need a clear IEP if you move to another town in your state or to another state altogether. In this scenario, the details matter even more because that new district is legally obligated to reasonably provide a comparable IEP to the one they just inherited.

What Your School District Isn't Telling You

We hate to be cynical about this, but your school district is unlikely to tell you it has chosen nebulous language on the IEP to be exactly that—nebulous. The document is designed to be specific and direct accountability. The school district won't tell you it would like to keep the language vague to give the district as much wiggle room as possible later when you're trying to hold it accountable. We've seen one too many measurement systems on IEP goals that are incomprehensible to almost everyone, and when asked, even the person who drafted the IEP can't articulate the rationale.

What Can You Do about It

Let's start with the IEP goals. Learn how to write SMART— Specific, Measurable, Action words, Results-oriented, and Time-bound—IEP goals.

Now sit down with a highlighter and mark up each and every single toothless word in the IEP goals. Beyond the IEP goals, call out toothless IEP language in the rest of the document. Start on page one and review the IEP section by section. Highlight every word or phrase that seems to have no real meaning or accountability. Ask yourself: Could someone who picks up this document understand what's supposed to happen in my child's program?

Next, call a working team meeting to share your concerns. Tell them you want the team to work through replacing all of the nebulous language with SMARTer language. This will be a process and require patience. Come to the meeting with all of your suggested changes. Once you have settled on the changes, call a full IEP team meeting to memorialize them. As an alternative, you can call a full IEP team meeting at the beginning and go through the process there. This will largely depend on the amount of information you need to cover and whether you or your team wants to meet before the full IEP meeting. The IEP can only be changed through an IEP team meeting, or through a written IEP amendment to the document properly signed by you and the district.

You would also be well served to document all of your concerns along the way. Here is a sample email as a starting place:

> Dear (insert principal or person with whom you communicate),
>
> I have been trying to understand my child's IEP better in the hope that I can be a more meaningful participant in the development of his/her IEP. After examining (insert name)'s goals and IEP, I realize that much of the language, including in the goals, is vague, subject to interpretation, or unclear to me. I would like to request a team meeting to review my concerns and suggestions for changes.

Please tell me how you would like to move forward. Do you want to have a working meeting or go straight to an IEP team meeting to hear my concerns and consider my proposed revisions? If the working meeting results in a consensus about the goals and changes to the IEP, we can develop an IEP amendment.

I look forward to hearing from you.

Many thanks,

(insert your name)

cc: Director of Special Education

Don't let vague wording impede your child's education. Make sure the IEP language is clear to you and everyone else who uses it.

28

Little-Understood IEP Essentials

Though you don't need to educate yourself to the point of becoming a professional special education advocate or attorney, there are essential elements of the IEP process that you *must* know. Here they are:

1. Prior Written Notice: What does this actually mean? It means that prior to any action being taken by the school district, parents are to be given written notice and this notice must be recorded on the state's IEP form. What kinds of actions? If you disagreed with the district's evaluation(s) and you requested an independent evaluation, the district is supposed to document its yes or no answer, along with its reason why, on Prior Written Notice (usually a section on the IEP form). If you have requested that your child have one hour of speech per week versus the half hour a week the district recommended, and the district said no to your request, the answer must be documented on Prior Written Notice. Why? Because if it's not in writing, it never happened. If you end up in a dispute with your district over your disagreement, it's hard to establish

there was a disagreement if it never made its way onto the paperwork.

Don't assume that the district is going to document your requests on Prior Written Notice. Get in the habit of asking that any request that requires a yes or no answer be documented on Prior Written Notice. Locate Prior Written Notice on your state's IEP form. Practice saying "I would like to request (insert request here) to be reflected on Prior Written Notice." Be sure that your district has recorded either its agreement to your request or its refusal of your request on Prior Written Notice. Check the forms when you receive them to be sure this change is actually reflected.

2. Addendums: When you receive the IEP paperwork and discover that you disagree with anything about the documentation, there is something you should know. You can write an addendum. An addendum can capture inaccuracies, discrepancies, omissions, and misstatements of the facts. Some discrepancies on IEPs are clerical and include typos or unintentional errors like stating that your child is five years old rather than six. These can be considered housekeeping issues and should be corrected with an addendum. They are important, but they are not likely to alter your child's IEP, the services he is getting, or how the services are delivered.

Other inaccuracies are far more important, like the omission of your request for services that were denied and not captured on Prior Written Notice or your parent concerns that were not included. It might be an accommodation you and the team discussed and agreed upon that wasn't captured. Conversely, there might be modifications

174

on the paperwork that were never discussed at the meeting and you didn't know your child was receiving, which may greatly alter your child's program. For example, parents often believe that their child was graded on the same criteria as the other students. Then, when they get the report card with all As, they wonder how their child did so well when he is struggling with basic skills. In this scenario, the child's IEP may have a modification that says he will be graded on his IEP, not on the general education curriculum.

So how do you write an addendum? Every state has different IEP paperwork, but you can follow general rules. Write an introduction to your addendum politely explaining that you have noticed inaccuracies, discrepancies, or omissions on the IEP and that you are submitting an addendum. The addendum itself should correlate with each section of the IEP so the person reading it can follow your logic. It can be narrative or a list. There is no right or wrong way to do it—just make sure it will make sense to the reader. Here are a couple of examples:

Recommendations: It states here that "Transition assessments will be conducted in the fall." This is an inaccurate statement. The team actually decided to start the assessments in the spring. In addition, please include the following recommendation that was omitted: "The team recommended considering an assistive technology evaluation at the next IEP team meeting."

Parent Input: Please include the following statement shared at the IEP meeting, but not listed here: "Parents shared that their son has not been sleeping well and would like the team to be aware that this might impact his performance at school." And "Parents are quite concerned about their son's behavior and shared their disappointment that he is hitting other students. They are also disappointed that the team had not conducted a Functional Behavior Assessment."

These are laborious to write and, frankly, not much fun. Always include language that makes it clear that your concerns or changes are not necessarily an exhaustive list but rather address the issues that jumped out at you the most. Finally, make sure you request that your addendum is attached to your child's educational record.

An addendum can start with an introductory email like this:

Dear (insert name),

I am in receipt of my child's IEP from (insert date). After reviewing it, I have noticed some discrepancies/omissions. Please consider the following an addendum to my child's IEP, attach this addendum to the IEP, and place a copy in all of his/her educational files maintained in the district.

Many thanks,

(insert your name)

cc: Director of Special Education

3. ESY: Some IEPs don't take summer vacations (as noted above but worth repeating here). We can't tell you how many times parents report that they didn't know their child could have been eligible for Extended School Year (ESY) services—and didn't even know what ESY services were. Not all students' IEPs will rise to the level where they may require extended school year services, but the IDEA requires the team to discuss and consider if your child requires them in order to receive a free appropriate public education (FAPE). Your IEP team should also discuss and consider what, if any, interaction your child will have in an ESY program with nondisabled peers. Some states require ESY to be discussed no later than a specific month in the school year. If ESY is discussed too late in the school year, and you disagree with the decision the team has made, you may not have enough time to exercise your right to dispute the district's decision. Make sure you discuss ESY early enough to allow yourself time to dispute the decision, if necessary.

Here is an email you can send to address the issue:

Dear (insert administrator's name),

I would like to bring a matter to your attention regarding consideration of extended school year services (ESY) for my child (insert name), who attends (insert school) in the (insert grade).

I have historically been in the position where my son's/daughter's school team either did not discuss

177

consideration of eligibility for ESY and/or when we did discussed it too late in the school year for me to make alternative plans, thereby not affording me the right to appeal the team's decision in a timely manner.

I believe my son/daughter has been denied a free appropriate public education (FAPE) by denying him/her ESY in the past. This school year I would like to hold an IEP team meeting in (insert month) to consider eligibility for ESY.

Many thanks,

(insert your name)

cc: Director of Special Education

4. Parent Input and Concerns: You are allowed to have input and concerns and the IEP team must consider them and any other information you provide about your child. Parents are supposed to be valued members of the team and your input and concerns are important to consider. The team doesn't have to agree with the parents' input and concerns; they belong to the parents and are not up for debate. If the team questions your contributions, say, "It's my understanding that one of the reasons that we, as parents, are required to be invited to this meeting is so that *our* input is considered by the team." If you have

provided information to the IEP team, make sure your input is documented on the IEP.

5. Para Educators: If your child has a paraprofessional or aide as a part of her special education services, take careful note of how that is documented. We often see situations where a student has an aide, but the aide is never mentioned on the IEP. We have seen paraprofessionals listed in an IEP to be provided "as needed," which can lead to a poor understanding of the role that person plays on your child's IEP. Does your child share a para with another child (or children)? Document the para's exact role on your child's IEP. Does your child's aide require ongoing training in a specific area as it relates to your child? Make sure the IEP captures the specific training that person requires, who is responsible for the training, and who ensures the fidelity of the services the para is delivering. Further, if you believe your child should have a para educator but your child's IEP team has refused your request, make sure you ask that your request and the reasons for it have been documented on Prior Written Notice, including an explanation of why the para has been denied by the school team. This denial gives you an opportunity to discuss understanding how your child functions throughout the school day without a para educator's assistance. Ask that data be collected to inform the team on the decision, including, if necessary, updated evaluations of your child's skills.

6. Nonacademic and extracurricular activities: If your child is going to participate in any nonacademic, extracurricular, school-sponsored activities, the team must

consider if your child will require any support in those areas as a part of their IEP. The Office of Civil Rights of the United States Department of Education (OCR) issued an excellent letter of guidance on January 25, 2013, which emphasizes the importance of this protection, and is a handy document to have with you in the IEP meeting for when it comes up. You can find it at www2.ed.gov/about/offices/list/ocr/letters/colleague -201301-504.pdf.

7. Revision of the IEP and assistive technology: Every time the IEP team revises your child's IEP, it must consider if your child requires assistive technology. The IDEA and its regulations state that the IEP team *must* consider "whether the child needs assistive technology devices and services." Technology has become an essential tool for all of us, and can make the difference for many students between being able to participate effectively in the general education environment or being left out of the mainstream. Don't let your IEP team ignore this important component of your child's program or save it for the end of the meeting as an afterthought.

What Your School District Isn't Telling You

The IDEA has a number of important requirements that go unnoticed, including all of the points noted above. Your school team may not even be aware of some of these requirements, but you should be and you should bring them to your team's attention.

What You Can Do about It

The only way you're ever going to be familiar enough with your rights to be able to use them effectively is if you stay current with them. This means reading statutes won't suffice. You may have to read the IDEA and the regulations and this book repeatedly. You will also need to attend trainings, conferences, and webinars and read news alerts about court cases and changes to legislation. You must be vigilant when it comes to your child's special education program. Just as we don't accept a "one and done" training for school teams, this is the beginning, not the end, of your advocacy education. If this aspect of the process is too daunting, you are probably going to have to resign yourself to the fact that you will need to bring in professional advocacy support for your child going forward.

29

Finding Your Advocacy Style

You are your child's best advocate. But the manner in which you advocate affects the outcome and the reputation you get while doing so. Your advocacy style matters. Parents need to keep in mind Bill Laviano's adage about out-of-district placements: "Kids don't get outplaced; parents do." By this he meant, very simply, that some school districts get so fed up with a parent that they will happily send that child to a private placement just so they don't have to deal with that parent anymore. Sad, but true. We are not suggesting you become this parent.

We have worked with parents who tell us that they can't speak at the IEP meeting because they are too intimated by the team, rendering them ineffective. On the opposite end of the spectrum, we have worked with parents who are larger than life and are overly forceful, rendering them equally ineffective in their advocacy efforts. We are not suggesting you become this parent.

Parents come in all types of advocacy styles. Know yours. What kind of an advocate are you? Are you meek, bossy, loud, overpowering, too polite, a bull in a china shop, or the parent who brings cookies to the IEP meeting? And how's that working for you?

Ask yourself if your advocacy style clashes with your team or someone on your team. Is your style getting your child an appropriate program? If so, you may not need to change a thing. If it isn't yielding the results you hoped for and you don't believe your child has an appropriate program, then it's time for you to review your style and make some decisions. You need to know your strengths and weaknesses as they relate to your advocacy efforts. Reflect back on some of the IEP team meetings you have had with your team. Which ones went well and why? Which ones went poorly and why? This analysis may help you identify your strengths and weaknesses as your child's advocate.

Your personal advocacy style should have absolutely no legal effect on the decisions made on behalf of your child. The reality is, however, that it does. Choose your advocacy style wisely.

What Your School District Isn't Telling You

Some school districts will genuinely encourage you to be the best advocate you can be for your child. They may provide training to families; continuing education in the form of speakers and presenters on disability and disability rights; and useful literature for parents. Some districts will incorporate regularly scheduled parent team meetings with you monthly. Others secretly hope that you take a back seat in the process, simply accepting what the IEP team recommends. It makes their lives so much easier.

What You Can Do about It

Know thyself seems a little too simplistic, but it really isn't. You need to know what you can realistically pull off when advocating for your child. We have many parents come to us and say, "I just can't do this," or "I'm too emotional to do this." We have families for whom English is their second language and lack confidence to advocate from a language perspective. Others admit they are too hot-headed and lack the ability to conduct themselves with decorum. We know you can't be objective about your own child; neither can we!

Who are you? Are you up to this challenge? Can you arm yourself with all of this information and conduct yourself politely and with grace? Most importantly: Are you being effective? This is truly the bottom line to consider when you review your advocacy style.

If you realize that you are not being effective, you may want to work with a special education advocate or attorney. As a special education advocate and attorney, we are often retained by parents who let us know that they simply haven't been effective in getting their child what they believe is appropriate and they need our help. They are able to recognize that their advocacy efforts haven't worked and they are ready for someone to step in to assist them. If you are at this stage, we encourage you to find advocates and attorneys in your state at COPAA.org (The Council of Parent Attorneys and Advocates) or by calling your state's special education department or Parent Advocacy Center. Your state's Parent Information and Training Center (http://www.parentcenterhub.org/find-your-center/) can also help.

30

Best-Kept Secrets

Parents advocating for their children with disabilities need access to many different resources. We've mentioned some in earlier chapters (which bear repeating here), and have others added here that can be tremendously powerful to use on your journey to getting a quality education for your child.

1. FERPA: Family Education Rights and Privacy Act. This federal law stipulates that your child's educational records are private and cannot be provided to just anyone without your permission (or that of your child when he reaches the age of majority). Think of it as the educational version of the HIPAA forms you sign in the doctor's office. In addition, under FERPA you are entitled to have access to these educational records. And this is where it becomes powerful. The very first thing we do when retained by parents is obtain all of the child's educational records. Then we have all report cards, progress reports, IEPs, evaluations, state testing results, incident reports, nurses visits, and virtually all other documentation of the child's history in school. You are also entitled to request the emails exchanged among the team

members about your child. This can be fascinating information and in some cases can prove an important concern or point you've been trying to make without success prior to getting your child's records. Familiarize yourself with FERPA. Also check your state records protections as well.

2. FOIA: Freedom of Information Act. This is a federal law (and again, there are many additional state protections in most states) known as a "sunshine law." The goal of the FOIA and other statutes like it is to ensure transparency in our governmental agencies and entities. This applies to how they spend their money, with whom they hold contracts, and when and how often they report information to state and federal governments. While the FOIA is not a statute that covers your child as an individual in terms of his records, there is still valuable information that you can obtain as a citizen by using the FOIA. For example: your school district has hired a consultant to work with it on programming for children with a certain disability. You think the consultant is biased and making recommendations the school district wants him to make. Under the FOIA, you can ask for a copy of the contract between the consultant and the district. If you discover that the consultant—who the school district describes as neutral—is getting paid six figures by that one particular school district to consult, you can call his bias into question. Or maybe you're wondering what your school district spends on special education legal fees every year while fighting with you over an additional half an hour a week of speech services. The FOIA can be your friend!

3. Ed.gov: This is the website for the United States Department of Education. Bookmark this site so you can look up the law and regulations surrounding special education, civil rights, school access, and more. It provides links to the essential OSERS (Office of Special Education and Rehabilitative Services), OSEP (Office of Special Education Programs) and OCR (Office for Civil Rights) and it is filled with a treasure trove of valuable information. It's hard for your school district to argue with the United States Department of Education!

4. COPAA: Council of Parent Attorneys and Advocates. This is the leading national voice on disability rights of students in the United States. The organization consists of professionals (attorneys, advocates, and related professionals), parents, and students. It hosts valuable listservs and an incredibly informative annual conference. You can find it at COPAA.org.

5. P&A: Protection and Advocacy. According to the National Disabilities Rights Network, or (NDRN), "P&A agencies have the authority to provide legal representation and other advocacy services, under all federal and state laws, to all people with disabilities (based on a system of priorities for services). All P&As maintain a presence in facilities that care for people with disabilities, where they monitor, investigate and attempt to remedy adverse conditions. These agencies also devote considerable resources to ensuring full access to inclusive educational programs, financial entitlements, healthcare, accessible housing and productive employment opportunities." What does this mean to you as a parent? It means

that you might get legal representation without having to pay a private lawyer.

6. Parent Training and Information Centers: The IDEA requires states to create these so that parents can have access to information about their rights. As with almost any agency, their quality can vary, but most will be more than happy to provide staff to speak with parents and help guide them through the process. Some have advocates who will attend IEP meetings with parents. These groups are often very aware of the movers and shakers (good and bad) in your state and can often give valuable insight into whether a professional evaluator you are considering has a good reputation.

7. Due process hearings and complaints: Parents who disagree with their school district's program for their child can pursue a due process hearing under the IDEA or can file a complaint with their state Department of Education. Many states publish the decisions online; reading them may give you valuable information.

8. Topic briefs and other guidance: Many states provide topic briefs, written guidance to school districts on everything from standards for summer services to what is and isn't lawful when determining criteria for Independent Educational Evaluations. Not only should you try to find what's published on your state's website, but if you're really motivated you can ask your state to send you any topic briefs it has issued.

9. SEPTOs and SEPTAs (Special Education Parent Teacher Organizations or Associations): Just like the PTA, there are PTAs for the community of students with disabilities.

These groups usually consist of parents who network with one another, meet regularly, and invite speakers to educate the parents in their community. If your town doesn't have one, we have an idea: start one!

10. Law clinics: We know all too well that access to affordable, quality professional advocacy is limited for most families. The average parent can't spend hundreds or even thousands of dollars on a private lawyer or advocate to secure services for their child. This is why we encourage parents to not only investigate Legal Aid and other similar types of programs, but to also look into whether a law school near them has a family law or similar clinic. These clinics provide supervised law students who can represent you. It's similar to the idea of a teaching hospital: you might get someone who's still learning, but everyone benefits and you generally don't have to pay for the service.

11. Par Assessment Toolkit App: Never again will you have to be in the dark when it comes to understanding an evaluation full of charts and data representing your child's functioning. The Par Assessment Toolkit —available for free at many app stores—has a handy bell curve, converts data, and has other tools to help you understand assessment. This is a must download!

12. Mailing lists and alerts: Register to receive alerts and updates from websites that focus on disabilities, both specific to your child's disability and those that provide information on the law and special education advocacy. In fact, registering to get alerts from state and federal agencies can be invaluable; you may find out about a

recent development from an email alert that even your child's special education team doesn't yet know. In addition to Ed.gov, which we've covered above, sign up for notices or email lists of resources you find online. Worst case scenario, you can unsubscribe later if it starts to annoy you or proves of little value.

13. YSER: YourSpecialEducationRights.com. We are partial to this one. Why? Because it's our site! YSER is a unique, video-based website that is free to parents, and we have hundreds of videos designed to educate parents about their special education rights. Some of our favorites are the mock IEP meetings where we interrupt the meeting to inform you of your rights in real time and our many series on important topics like mental health and bullying. Check us out at www.YourSpecialEducationRights. com.

There are many resources available online to families, and we encourage you to investigate them.

References

Page 1: Individuals with Disabilities Education Act (IDEA), 20 USC 1400 et. seq.

Page 7: Section 504 of the Rehabilitation Act of 1973, 29 USC 701.

Page 11: Individuals with Disabilities Education Act (IDEA), 20 USC 1414(d)(1)(B).

Page 27–29: Section 504 of the Rehabilitation Act of 1973, 29 USC 701.

Page 29: "How to Start a Special Education PTA": http://www.pta. org/parents/content.cfm?ItemNumber=2100.

Page 32: Individuals with Disabilities Education Act (IDEA), 20 USC 1412 (a)(5).

Page 55: Public Act 15.5, Section 277.

Pages 56–58: IDEA Regulations, 34 CFR 300.156(b) [20 U.S.C. 1412(a)(14)(B)].

Page 58: Paraprofessional Requirements, No Child Left Behind Act: https://www2.ed.gov/policy/elsec/guid/paraletterjd42602.doc.

Page 65: Report of the Office of the Child Advocate on the shooting at Sandy Hook Elementary School: http://www.ct.gov/oca/lib/oca/ sandyhook11212014.pdf.

Page 66: "Fact Sheet: Violence and Mental Illness," American Psychiatric Association, Washington, DC: "People with psychiatric disabilities are far more likely to be victims than perpetrators of violent crime (Appleby, et al., 2001). People with severe mental illnesses, schizophrenia, bipolar disorder or psychosis, are 2 ½ times more likely to be attacked, raped or mugged than the general population (Hiday, et al.,1999)."

People with Asperger's syndrome are no more likely than the general population to commit a crime; those with "classic autism" were less likely than other people to commit crimes. See Mouridsen, S.E., Rich, B., Isager, T., and Nedergaard, N.J. (2008). "Pervasive Developmental Disorders and Criminal Behavior: A Case Control Study." *International Journal of Offender Therapy and Comparative Criminology* 52:196.

Page 69: Josh Kovner, "Lanza's Psychiatrist Later Surrendered License After 'Sexual Relationship' With Patient," *Hartford Courant*, Dec. 30, 2012.

Page 75: Section 504 of the Rehabilitation Act of 1973, 29 USC 701.

Page 108: US Department of Education Office for Civil Rights: https://www2.ed.gov/about/offices/list/ocr/index.html.

Page 110: Daniel R. R. v. State Board of Education, 874 F.2d 1036, 1041 (5th Cir. 1988).

Page 118: OSEP Policy Documents, including letter to Mamas https://www2.ed.gov/policy/speced/guid/idea/letters/revpolicy/tpedpl.html.

Page 125: IDEA Regulations, 34 CFR 300.322.

Page 135: IDEA Regulations, 34 CFR 300.1.

References

Page 136: IDEA Regulations, 34 CFR 300.43.

Page 137: Naviance: https://naviance.com.

Page 145: "US Department of Education IEP Guide": https://www2. ed.gov/parents/needs/speced/iepguide/index.html?exp=0.

Page 159: Council of Parent Attorneys and Advocates, Inc.: www. COPAA.org.

Page 159: "COPAA Guidelines for Choosing an Advocate": http:// www.copaa.org/?page=GuidelinesAdv.

Page 187: Family Educational Rights and Privacy Act (FERPA): https://www2.ed.gov/policy/gen/guid/fpco/ferpa/index.html?src=rn/.

Page 188: Freedom of Information Act (FOIA): https://www.foia.gov.

Page 192: Our website: www.YourSpecialEducationRights.com.

Acknowledgments

We want to start by thanking Skyhorse for believing in this book and the importance of sharing it with parents and professionals. In particular, we thank Louis Conte, Susan Randol, and Olga Greco at Skyhorse for holding our hands as we meandered our way through our first publishing experience!

We have wanted to write this book for years, and at least once a week, a parent with whom we work says, "You should write a book about this stuff!" When we finally decided to actually write it, we mentioned it to our good friend, website manager, and warrior mom Babs Distinti. Since Babs is one of those people who knows everyone and everything, she reminded us that fellow Connecticut parent Kim Stagliano published her books through Skyhorse. One thing led to another, and here we are! We want to thank Babs and Kim for being a part of carving the path to publishing for us.

We peek behind the scenes of the special education system with the sole purpose of helping parents of children who have special education needs understand the barriers that often arise in this multilayered, complicated landscape. Those barriers often result in a deprivation of appropriate services for children, which means lost skills and reduced outcomes. Despite this, we are products of the public school system; we believe in it, and we thank our public school teachers for the hard work we know they do every single day. We write this book in the hope that public school administrators, educators, and other stakeholders will understand the perspective of parents and those of us in the special education advocacy community.

We should all have the same goal: a quality education for *all* children.

To the families with whom we work, who have allowed us to share parts of their stories: we cannot thank you enough. You inspire us, make us laugh, make us cry, and remind us each and every day why we do this.

To our friends, thank you for understanding how important this book is to us and for supporting us.

More personally, we want to thank our families. Jen thanks her girls, Emmy and Marisa, who make her laugh and think every day. Julie thanks her husband, Steve, and her boys, Nick and Alex, who support her without question. Neither of us would have finished this book without your steadfast support and understanding. Your tolerance for our absence is a great testament of your love for us, and your belief in our mission. We thank you, and we love you.

To our siblings: Jen wishes to thank Kristin Laviano-Rhodes, Jon Rhodes, Lauren King, Jeff King, and Katie Laviano. Your support, understanding, and humor are a constant. Julie thanks her brother, Bob, for encouraging her and making her laugh and her sister, Donna, for supporting her in every way. We love you and thank you for knowing this work is so important to us.

To our parents: To Jen's mom, Donna Laviano, thank you for loving me, and for always correcting my grammar; it came in handy during the writing of this book! To Julie's parents, Janet and Howard: you are the best parents a girl could ask for. Thank you for your love and support.

To the late Bill Laviano: there are no words. You took them all. Every day you inspire each of us and all of us, and we love you and know that you are somewhere, picking a fight that's worth picking, and that you're winning.

Index